BONUS

POPULARITY EXPLOSION

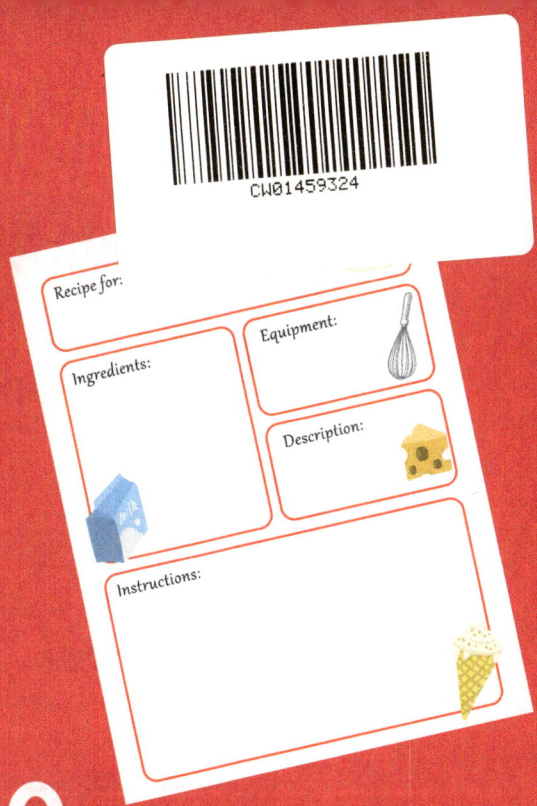

SAY GOODBYE TO KITCHEN STRESS

HELLO TO EFFORTLESS COOKING

1800 Days Daily Instant Pot Recipes with Full-colour Pictures, Simplify Your Kitchen Routine and Enjoy Nourishing and Quality Meals

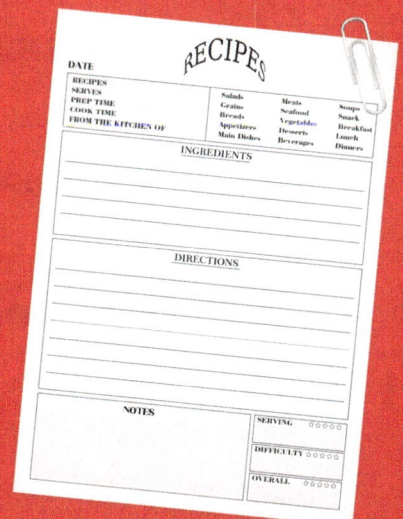

Recipe for:

Equipment:

Ingredients:

Description:

Instructions:

RECIPES

DATE
RECIPES
SERVES   Salads   Meats   Soups
PREP TIME   Gratins   Seafood   Snack
COOK TIME   Breads   Vegetable   Breakfast
FROM THE KITCHEN OF   Appetizers   Desserts   Lunch
                Main Dishes   Beverages   Dinners

INGREDIENTS

DIRECTIONS

NOTES

SERVING
DIFFICULTY
OVERALL

CONTENTS

INTRODUCTION

Greetings, and welcome to the world of culinary exploration as presented in the Instant Pot Cookbook. I'm Helen J. Hill, and it's my immense pleasure to embark on this flavorful journey with you. With a culinary career spanning over two decades, I've had the privilege of working in renowned restaurants and fine dining establishments. These experiences have not only fueled my passion for creating exceptional dishes but have also instilled in me an unwavering commitment to combining taste and health in every meal.

The creation of this cookbook was born out of my deep appreciation for the revolutionary kitchen appliance known as the Instant Pot. As a chef, I was immediately captivated by its ability to streamline cooking processes, reduce the time spent in the kitchen, and, most importantly, enhance the flavors of every dish it touches. My purpose in crafting this cookbook is twofold. Firstly, I aim to share a meticulously curated collection of recipes, specifically designed to unlock the full potential of the Instant Pot. These recipes cater to individuals and families seeking a wide array of dishes that are not only quick and easy but also nutritious and packed with flavor. Secondly, beyond the sumptuous recipes, I'm dedicated to empowering you with the knowledge and techniques to master this versatile appliance, regardless of your culinary expertise.

In these pages, you'll find a medley of dishes, from time-honored classics to innovative creations, all harmoniously suited to the Instant Pot. My mission is to inspire both novice and experienced cooks alike, encouraging you to explore the remarkable world of pressure cooking. Together, we'll unravel the endless possibilities and culinary delights this appliance has to offer, making meal preparation not only convenient but also a truly enjoyable and wholesome experience. So, as we embark on this culinary adventure, let the Instant Pot Cookbook be your trusty companion, guiding you toward a world of flavors, convenience, and culinary mastery. Welcome, and let's get started on this delicious journey together.

Helen J. Hill

Tips to be energized every day

1. Morning Exercise: Start with a quick workout.

2. Stay Hydrated: Drink water for alertness.

3. Balanced Nutrition: Eat protein, fats, and carbs.

4. Short Breaks: Stretch and breathe.

5. Positive Affirmations: Boost your mindset.

6. Power Naps: A quick recharge.

7. Sunlight Exposure: Mood and rhythm.

8. Deep Breathing: Stress reduction.

9. Socialize: Connect for energy.

10. Declutter: Organize for focus.

Breakfast

Breakfast

Peanut Butter And Banana Oatmeal

Servings:2

Cooking Time: 7 Minutes

Ingredients:

- 1 cup old-fashioned oats
- 1 ¼ cups water
- 1 large ripe banana, peeled and mashed
- 1 tablespoon packed light brown sugar
- ¼ teaspoon vanilla extract
- ¼ teaspoon ground cinnamon
- ⅛ teaspoon salt
- 2 tablespoons crunchy peanut butter

Directions:

1. In the Instant Pot, add oats, water, banana, brown sugar, vanilla, cinnamon, and salt. Stir to combine. Lock lid.
2. Press the Manual or Pressure Cook button and adjust time to 7 minutes. When timer beeps, let pressure release naturally until float valve drops. Unlock lid.
3. Stir in peanut butter, then spoon oatmeal into two bowls. Serve warm.

Pecan Chocolate Chip Breakfast Oats

Servings:2

Cooking Time: 7 Minutes

Ingredients:

- 1 cup old-fashioned oats
- 1 cup water
- 1 cup whole milk
- ¼ teaspoon vanilla extract
- 2 tablespoons packed light brown sugar
- 2 tablespoons chopped pecans
- ⅛ teaspoon salt
- 2 tablespoons mini chocolate chips

Directions:

1. In the Instant Pot, add oats, water, milk, vanilla, brown sugar, pecans, and salt. Stir to combine. Lock lid.
2. Press the Manual or Pressure Cook button and adjust time to 7 minutes. When timer beeps, quick-release pressure until float valve drops. Unlock lid.
3. Stir oatmeal, then spoon into two bowls and garnish with chocolate chips. Serve warm.

Sunday Brunch Sausage Gravy

Servings:10

Cooking Time: 10 Minutes

Ingredients:

- 2 tablespoons butter
- 1 pound ground pork sausage
- 1 small sweet onion, peeled and diced
- ¼ cup chicken broth
- ¼ cup all-purpose flour
- 1½ cups heavy cream
- ½ teaspoon sea salt
- 1 tablespoon ground black pepper

Directions:

1. Press the Sauté button on the Instant Pot. Add butter and heat until melted. Add pork sausage and onion. Stir-fry 3–5 minutes until onions are translucent. The pork will still be a little pink in places. Add chicken broth. Lock lid.
2. Press the Manual button and adjust time to 1 minute. When the timer beeps, quick-release the pressure until the float valve drops and then unlock the lid. Whisk in flour, cream, salt, and pepper.
3. Press the Keep Warm button and let the gravy sit for about 5–10 minutes to allow the sauce to thicken. Remove from heat and serve warm.

Cinnamon Roll Doughnut Holes

Servings:14

Cooking Time: 16 Minutes

Ingredients:

- 1 package Krusteaz Cinnamon Roll Supreme Mix (includes icing packet)
- 6 tablespoons unsalted butter, melted
- ½ cup cold water
- ¼ cup chopped pecans
- 1 cup water

Directions:

1. In a medium bowl, combine dry mix, butter, and ½ cup cold water. Fold in pecans. Spoon half of batter into a greased seven-hole silicone egg mold. If your egg mold has a silicone top, use this. If your egg mold came with a plastic top, do not use. Instead, cover with aluminum foil.
2. Add 1 cup water to the Instant Pot and insert steam rack. Place egg mold on steam rack. Lock lid.
3. Press the Manual or Pressure Cook button and adjust time to 8 minutes. When timer beeps, quick-release pressure until float valve drops. Unlock lid.
4. Pop doughnut holes out of egg mold and repeat with remaining batter.
5. When doughnut holes are cooled, mix icing packet with 1 ½ tablespoons water and dip doughnut holes into glaze to cover. Serve.

Chocolate Banana French Toast Casserole

Servings:4

Cooking Time: 20 Minutes

Ingredients:

- 4 cups cubed bread, dried out overnight, divided
- 2 bananas, peeled and sliced
- 4 tablespoons chocolate syrup, divided
- 2 cups whole milk
- 3 large eggs
- 1 teaspoon vanilla extract
- ¼ cup pure maple syrup
- Pinch of ground nutmeg
- Pinch of sea salt
- 3 tablespoons butter, cut into 3 pats
- 1 cup water

Directions:

1. Grease a 7-cup glass dish. Add 2 cups bread. Arrange banana slices in an even layer over bread. Drizzle 2 tablespoons chocolate syrup over bananas. Add remaining 2 cups bread. Set aside.
2. In a medium bowl, whisk together milk, eggs, vanilla, maple syrup, nutmeg, and salt. Pour over bread; place pats of butter on top.
3. Pour water into Instant Pot. Set trivet in Instant Pot. Place glass dish on top of trivet. Lock lid.
4. Press the Manual button and adjust time to 20 minutes. When the timer beeps, quick-release pressure until float valve drops and then unlock lid.
5. Remove glass bowl from the Instant Pot. Transfer to a rack until cooled. Top with remaining 2 tablespoons chocolate. Serve warm.

Banana Nut Muffins

Servings:6

Cooking Time: 9 Minutes

Ingredients:

- 1 ¼ cups all-purpose baking flour
- 2 teaspoons baking powder
- ½ teaspoon baking soda
- ⅛ teaspoon salt
- ½ teaspoon vanilla extract
- 3 tablespoons unsalted butter, melted
- 2 large eggs
- ¼ cup granulated sugar
- 2 medium ripe bananas, peeled and mashed with a fork
- ¼ cup chopped walnuts
- 1 cup water

Directions:

1. Grease six silicone cupcake liners.
2. In a large bowl, combine flour, baking powder, baking soda, and salt.
3. In a medium bowl, combine vanilla, butter, eggs, sugar, and bananas.
4. Pour wet ingredients from medium bowl into large bowl with dry ingredients. Gently combine ingredients. Do not overmix. Fold in walnuts, then spoon mixture into prepared cupcake liners.
5. Add water to the Instant Pot and insert steam rack. Place cupcake liners on top. Lock lid.
6. Press the Manual or Pressure Cook button and adjust time to 9 minutes. When timer beeps, quick-release pressure until float valve drops. Unlock lid.
7. Remove muffins from pot and set aside to cool 30 minutes. Serve.

Smoked Salmon & Egg Muffins

Servings: 2

Cooking Time: 15 Minutes

Ingredients:

- 4 beaten eggs
- 2 salmon slices, chopped
- 4 tbsp mozzarella, shredded
- 1 green onion, chopped

Directions:

1. Beat eggs, salmon, mozzarella cheese, and onion in a bowl. Share into ramekins. Pour 1 cup of water into your Instant Pot and fit in a trivet.
2. Place the tins on top of the trivet and seal the lid. Select Manual and cook for 8 minutes on High pressure. Once done, let sit for 2 minutes, then perform a quick pressure release and unlock the lid. Serve immediately.

Speedy Soft-boiled Eggs

Servings: 4

Cooking Time: 10 Minutes

Ingredients:

- 4 large eggs
- Salt and pepper to taste

Directions:

1. To the pressure cooker, add 1 cup of water and place a wire rack. Place eggs on it. Seal the lid, press Steam, and cook for 3 minutes on High Pressure. Do a quick release.
2. Allow to cool in an ice bath. Peel the eggs and season with salt and pepper before serving.

California Frittata Bake

Servings:4

Cooking Time: 10 Minutes

Ingredients:

- 4 large eggs
- 4 large egg whites
- ½ teaspoon sea salt
- ¼ teaspoon ground black pepper
- ¼ cup chopped fresh basil
- ½ cup chopped spinach
- 2 small Roma tomatoes, diced
- 1 medium avocado, pitted and diced
- ¼ cup grated Gruyère cheese
- 1 tablespoon avocado oil
- 1 pound ground chicken
- 1 small onion, peeled and diced
- 1 cup water

Directions:

1. In a medium bowl, whisk together eggs, egg whites, salt, and pepper. Add basil, spinach, tomatoes, avocado, and cheese. Set aside.
2. Press the Sauté button on Instant Pot. Heat the avocado oil and stir-fry chicken and onion for approximately 5 minutes or until chicken is no longer pink.
3. Transfer cooked mixture to a 7-cup greased glass dish and set aside to cool. Once cool pour whisked eggs over the chicken mixture and stir to combine.
4. Place trivet in Instant Pot. Pour in water. Place dish with egg mixture onto trivet. Lock lid.
5. Press the Manual button and adjust time to 5 minutes. When the timer beeps, let pressure release naturally until the float valve drops and then unlock the lid.
6. Remove dish from the Instant Pot and set aside for 5–10 minutes to allow the eggs to set. Slice and serve.

Ham And Swiss Muffin Frittatas

Servings:3

Cooking Time: 15 Minutes

Ingredients:

- 1 tablespoon olive oil
- ¼ cup small-diced ham
- ¼ cup diced red bell pepper, seeded
- 4 large eggs
- ½ teaspoon sea salt
- ½ teaspoon ground black pepper
- ¼ cup shredded Swiss cheese
- 1 cup water

Directions:

1. Press the Sauté button on Instant Pot. Heat olive oil. Add ham and bell pepper and stir-fry 3–5 minutes until peppers are tender. Transfer mixture to a small bowl to cool.
2. In a medium bowl, whisk together eggs, salt, pepper, and Swiss cheese. Stir in cooled ham mixture.
3. Place trivet into Instant Pot. Pour in water. Place steamer basket on trivet.
4. Distribute egg mixture evenly among 6 silicone muffin cups. Carefully place cups on steamer basket. Lock lid.
5. Press the Manual button and adjust time to 8 minutes. When timer beeps, quick-release pressure until float valve drops and then unlock lid.
6. Remove frittatas and serve warm.

Sausage And Sweet Potato Hash

Servings:4

Cooking Time: 10 Minutes

Ingredients:

- ½ pound ground pork sausage
- 1 large sweet potato, peeled and grated
- 1 small yellow onion, peeled and diced
- 2 cloves garlic, peeled and minced
- 1 medium green bell pepper, seeded and diced
- 1 tablespoon Italian seasoning
- ½ teaspoon salt
- ½ teaspoon ground black pepper
- 2 cups water

Directions:

1. Press the Sauté button on the Instant Pot. Stir-fry sausage, sweet potato, onion, garlic, bell pepper, Italian seasoning, salt, and black pepper 3–5 minutes until onions are translucent. Press the Cancel button.
2. Transfer mixture to a greased 7-cup glass baking dish.
3. Add water to the Instant Pot and insert steam rack. Place dish on steam rack. Lock lid.
4. Press the Manual or Pressure Cook button and adjust time to 5 minutes. When timer beeps, quick-release pressure until float valve drops. Unlock lid.
5. Remove dish from the Instant Pot. Spoon hash onto plates and serve.

Honey Butternut Squash Cake Oatmeal

Servings: 4

Cooking Time: 35 Minutes

Ingredients:

- 3 ½ cups coconut milk
- 1 cup steel-cut oats
- 8 oz butternut squash, grated
- ½ cup sultanas
- 1/3 cup honey
- ¾ tsp ground ginger
- ½ tsp salt
- ½ tsp orange zest
- ¼ tsp ground nutmeg
- ¼ cup walnuts, chopped
- ½ tsp vanilla extract
- ½ tsp sugar

Directions:

1. In the cooker, mix sultanas, orange zest, ginger, milk, honey, butternut squash, salt, oats, and nutmeg. Seal the lid and cook on High Pressure for 12 minutes. Do a natural release for 10 minutes. Into the oatmeal, stir in the vanilla extract and sugar. Top with walnuts and serve.

Pumpkin Muffins

Servings:6

Cooking Time: 9 Minutes

Ingredients:

- 1 ¼ cups all-purpose flour
- 2 teaspoons baking powder
- ½ teaspoon baking soda
- 1 teaspoon pumpkin pie spice
- ⅛ teaspoon salt
- ¼ cup pumpkin purée
- ½ teaspoon vanilla extract
- 1 tablespoon unsalted butter, melted
- 2 large eggs
- ⅓ cup packed light brown sugar
- 1 cup water

Directions:

1. Grease six silicone cupcake liners.
2. In a large bowl, combine flour, baking powder, baking soda, pumpkin pie spice, and salt.
3. In a medium bowl, combine pumpkin purée, vanilla, butter, eggs, and brown sugar.
4. Pour wet ingredients from medium bowl into large bowl with dry ingredients. Gently combine ingredients. Do not overmix. Spoon mixture into prepared cupcake liners.
5. Add water to the Instant Pot and insert steam rack. Place cupcake liners on top. Lock lid.
6. Press the Manual or Pressure Cook button and adjust time to 9 minutes. When timer beeps, quick-release pressure until float valve drops. Unlock lid.
7. Remove muffins from pot and set aside to cool 30 minutes. Serve.

Tofu Hash Brown Breakfast

Servings: 4

Cooking Time: 21 Minutes

Ingredients:

- 1 cup tofu cubes
- 2 cups frozen hash browns
- 8 beaten eggs
- 1 cup shredded cheddar
- ¼ cup milk
- Salt and pepper to taste

Directions:

1. Set your Instant Pot to Sauté. Place in tofu and cook until browned on all sides, about 4 minutes. Add in hash brown and cook for 2 minutes. Beat eggs, cheddar cheese, milk, salt, and pepper in a bowl and pour over hash brown. Seal the lid, select Manual, and cook for 5 minutes on High. Once done, perform a quick pressure release. Cut into slices before serving.

Grandma's Country Gravy

Servings: 6

Cooking Time: 16 Minutes

Ingredients:

- 2 tablespoons unsalted butter
- 1 pound ground pork sausage
- 1 small sweet onion, peeled and diced
- ¼ cup chicken broth
- ¼ cup all-purpose flour
- 1 ½ cups heavy cream
- ½ teaspoon salt
- 1 tablespoon ground black pepper

Directions:

1. Press the Sauté button on the Instant Pot. Add butter and heat until melted. Add sausage and onion and stir-fry 3–5 minutes until onions are translucent. The pork will still be a little pink in places. Add broth. Press the Cancel button. Lock lid.
2. Press the Manual or Pressure Cook button and adjust time to 1 minute. When timer beeps, quick-release pressure until float valve drops. Unlock lid. Whisk in flour, cream, salt, and pepper.
3. Press the Keep Warm button and let the gravy sit about 5–10 minutes to allow to thicken. Remove from heat. Serve warm.

Tex-mex Breakfast

Servings: 4

Cooking Time: 10 Minutes

Ingredients:

- 6 large eggs
- ½ teaspoon sea salt
- ¼ teaspoon ground black pepper
- ⅛ teaspoon chili powder
- ½ cup shredded Cheddar cheese
- 1 small Roma tomato, diced
- 2 tablespoons butter
- 2 small Yukon gold potatoes, grated
- 2 cups cubed cooked ham
- 1 small onion, peeled and diced
- 1 small jalapeño, seeded and diced
- ½ cup sliced button mushrooms
- 2 cups water

Directions:

1. In a medium bowl, whisk together eggs, salt, pepper, and chili powder. Stir in cheese and tomato. Set aside.
2. Press the Sauté button on Instant Pot. Heat the butter and stir-fry potatoes, ham, onion, jalapeño, and mushrooms for approximately 5 minutes until the potatoes are tender and onions are translucent.
3. Transfer cooked mixture to a 7-cup greased glass dish. Pour whisked eggs over the potato mixture.
4. Place trivet in Instant Pot. Pour in water. Place dish with egg mixture onto trivet. Lock lid.
5. Press the Manual button and adjust time to 5 minutes. When timer beeps, quick-release pressure until float valve drops and then unlock lid.
6. Remove dish from the Instant Pot. Let sit at room temperature for 5–10 minutes to allow the eggs to set. Slice and serve warm.

Blueberry-oat Muffins

Servings: 6

Cooking Time: 9 Minutes

Ingredients:

- 1 cup all-purpose baking flour
- ¼ cup old-fashioned oats
- 2 teaspoons baking powder
- ½ teaspoon baking soda
- ⅛ teaspoon salt
- ½ teaspoon vanilla extract
- 3 tablespoons unsalted butter, melted
- 2 large eggs
- 4 tablespoons granulated sugar
- ⅓ cup blueberries
- 1 cup water

Directions:

1. Grease six silicone cupcake liners.
2. In a large bowl, combine flour, oats, baking powder, baking soda, and salt.
3. In a medium bowl, combine vanilla, butter, eggs, and sugar.
4. Pour wet ingredients from medium bowl into the bowl with dry ingredients. Gently combine ingredients. Do not overmix. Fold in blueberries, then spoon mixture into prepared cupcake liners.
5. Add water to the Instant Pot and insert steam rack. Place cupcake liners on top. Lock lid.
6. Press the Manual or Pressure Cook button and adjust time to 9 minutes. When timer beeps, quick-release pressure until float valve drops. Unlock lid.
7. Remove muffins from pot and set aside to cool 30 minutes. Serve.

Spinach & Feta Pie With Cherry Tomatoes

Servings: 2

Cooking Time: 35 Minutes

Ingredients:

- 4 eggs
- Salt and pepper to taste
- ½ cup heavy cream
- 1 cup cherry tomatoes, halved
- 1 cup baby spinach
- 1 spring onion, chopped
- ¼ cup feta, crumbled
- 1 tbsp parsley, chopped

Directions:

1. Grease a baking dish with cooking spray and add in the spinach and onion. In a bowl, whisk the eggs, heavy cream, salt, and pepper. Pour over the spinach and arrange the cherry tomato on top. Sprinkle with the feta.
2. Add a cup of water to the Instant Pot and insert a trivet. Place the dish on the trivet. Seal the lid, press Manual, and cook on High pressure for 15 minutes. Release pressure naturally for 10 minutes. Scatter parsley to serve.

Trail Mix Oatmeal

Servings: 2

Cooking Time: 10 Minutes

Ingredients:

- 1 cup steel-cut oats
- 1½ cups water
- 2 teaspoons butter
- 1 cup freshly squeezed orange juice
- 1 tablespoon dried cranberries
- 1 tablespoon raisins
- 1 tablespoon chopped dried apricots
- 2 tablespoons pure maple syrup
- ¼ teaspoon ground cinnamon
- 2 tablespoons chopped pecans
- Pinch of salt

Directions:

1. Add all ingredients to the Instant Pot bowl and stir to combine. Lock lid.
2. Press the Manual button and adjust time to 10 minutes. When timer beeps, quick-release pressure until float valve drops and then unlock lid.
3. Stir oatmeal. Spoon the cooked oats into two bowls. Serve warm.

Appetizers, Soups & Sides

Appetizers, Soups & Sides

Chorizo & Bean Soup

Servings: 6

Cooking Time: 55 Minutes

Ingredients:

- 2 tbsp olive oil
- ¾ lb chorizo sausage, sliced
- 1 cup white beans, soaked
- 1 sweet pepper, sliced
- 14 oz can diced tomatoes
- 1 clove garlic, minced
- 1 onion, diced
- ½ tsp dried oregano
- 1 tsp chili powder
- 6 cups chicken broth

Directions:

1. Warm the olive oil in your Instant Pot on Sauté. Add in onion, garlic, chorizo, sweet pepper, chili powder, and oregano and cook for 4-5 minutes. Stir in chicken broth, tomatoes, and white bean and seal the lid. Select Manual and cook for 30 minutes. Once ready, perform a quick pressure release and let sit for 10 minutes. Serve warm.

Down-home Rainbow Chard

Servings:6

Cooking Time: 8 Minutes

Ingredients:

- 2 bunches rainbow chard, chopped (spines removed)
- 1 small yellow onion, peeled and diced
- ¼ cup apple cider vinegar
- 1 teaspoon hot sauce
- 1 smoked ham hock
- 1 cup chicken broth
- ½ teaspoon granulated sugar
- ½ teaspoon salt
- ¼ teaspoon ground black pepper

Directions:

1. Place all ingredients in the Instant Pot. Lock lid.
2. Press the Manual or Pressure Cook button and adjust time to 8 minutes. When timer beeps, let pressure release naturally until float valve drops. Unlock lid.
3. Flake off ham from bone and discard bone. Stir to incorporate ingredients.
4. Transfer to a serving dish and serve warm.

Parsley Creamy Tomato Soup

Servings: 4

Cooking Time: 50 Minutes

Ingredients:

- 2 lb tomatoes, diced
- 1 cup canned white beans
- 1 small onion, diced
- 2 garlic cloves, crushed
- 1 cup heavy cream
- 1 cup vegetable broth
- ½ tsp sugar
- Salt and pepper to taste
- 2 tbsp olive oil
- 2 tbsp parsley, chopped

Directions:

1. Warm oil on Sauté. Stir-fry onion and garlic for 2 minutes. Add tomatoes, beans, broth, 3 cups of water, parsley, salt, pepper, and a little bit of sugar to balance the bitterness. Seal the lid and cook on Soup/Broth for 30 minutes on High Pressure. Release the pressure naturally for 10 minutes. Carefully unlock the lid. Top with a dollop of heavy cream and serve.

Spicy Pumpkin Soup

Servings: 4

Cooking Time: 25 Minutes

Ingredients:

- 2 tbsp butter
- 1 Vidalia onion, chopped
- 2 garlic cloves, chopped
- 2 carrots, diced
- 1 lb pumpkin, peeled, diced
- ½ tsp thyme
- 1 tsp cumin seeds
- 1 tbsp hot curry paste
- 4 cups vegetable broth
- Salt and pepper to taste
- 1 cup heavy cream
- 2 tbsp cilantro, chopped

Directions:

1. Melt the butter in your Instant Pot on Sauté. Add in onion, garlic, carrots, salt, and pepper and cook for 3 minutes. Stir in cumin seeds, thyme, hot curry paste, and pumpkin for 2 minutes and pour in vegetable broth.
2. Seal the lid, select Manual, and cook for 10 minutes on High. When ready, perform a quick pressure release. Blend the soup using an immersion blender and stir in heavy cream. Top with cilantro to serve.

Thai Coconut Carrot Soup

Servings: 6

Cooking Time: 25 Minutes

Ingredients:

- 1 tablespoon coconut oil
- 1 small onion, peeled and diced
- 1 pound carrots, peeled and diced
- 2 cloves garlic, minced
- 1 tablespoon Thai red curry paste
- 4 cups vegetable broth
- 1 teaspoon honey
- 1 cup canned coconut milk
- 1 tablespoon fresh lime juice
- ¼ teaspoon red pepper flakes
- 1 teaspoon sea salt
- ½ teaspoon ground black pepper
- ¼ cup julienned fresh basil, plus 3 tablespoons for garnish

Directions:

1. Press the Sauté button on the Instant Pot and heat the coconut oil. Add the onion and carrots. Sauté for 3–5 minutes until onions are translucent. Add the garlic and curry paste. Continue to sauté for 1 minute. Add remaining ingredients, except 3 tablespoons basil. Lock lid.
2. Press the Soup button and adjust time to 20 minutes. When timer beeps, let pressure release naturally for 10 minutes. Quick-release any additional pressure until float valve drops and then unlock lid.
3. In the Instant Pot, purée soup with an immersion blender, or use a stand blender and purée in batches.
4. Ladle into bowls, garnish each bowl with ½ tablespoon basil, and serve warm.

Split Pea Soup With Ham

Servings: 4

Cooking Time: 35 Minutes

Ingredients:

- 1 tablespoon olive oil
- 1 large sweet onion, peeled and diced
- 2 medium stalks celery, diced
- 2 large carrots, peeled and diced
- 1 ½ cups dried green split peas, rinsed
- 5 cups chicken broth
- 1 teaspoon Italian seasoning
- 1 pound smoked ham hock
- ½ teaspoon salt
- ½ teaspoon ground black pepper

Directions:

1. Press the Sauté button on the Instant Pot and heat oil. Add onion, celery, and carrots. Sauté 3–5 minutes until onions are translucent. Add split peas, broth, Italian seasoning, ham hock, salt, and pepper. Press the Cancel button. Lock lid.
2. Press the Soup button and let cook for the default time of 30 minutes. When timer beeps, release pressure naturally for 5 minutes. Quick-release any additional pressure until float valve drops. Unlock lid. Pull ham off of the bone and chop ham into soup.
3. Ladle soup into four bowls. Serve warm.

Hazelnut Brussels Sprouts With Parmesan

Servings: 4

Cooking Time: 15 Minutes

Ingredients:

- 1 lb Brussels sprouts, halved
- 2 tbsp butter
- 2 garlic cloves, minced
- ¼ cup hazelnuts, chopped
- ½ tsp thyme
- ¼ cup grated Parmesan cheese
- Salt and pepper to taste

Directions:

1. Pour 1 cup of water into your Instant Pot and fit in a steamer basket. Place in the sprouts halves and seal the lid. Select Manual and cook for 3 minutes on High.
2. Once ready, perform a quick pressure release. Unlock the lid. Clean the pot and melt the butter on Sauté. Add in Brussels sprouts and garlic and Sauté for 2-3 minutes, stirring occasionally. Season with salt, pepper, and thyme and mix in hazelnuts. Serve topped with Parmesan cheese.

Steamed Artichokes With Lemon-garlic Yogurt Sauce

Servings:6

Cooking Time: 5 Minutes

Ingredients:

- Yogurt Sauce
- ¼ cup plain Greek yogurt
- Juice and zest of ½ medium lemon
- 3 cloves garlic, peeled and minced
- 1 tablespoon Dijon mustard
- ⅛ teaspoon salt
- Steamed Artichokes
- 6 medium artichokes
- 1 cup water
- 1 teaspoon salt

Directions:

1. In a small bowl, whisk together yogurt sauce ingredients. Refrigerate until ready to use.
2. Clean artichokes by clipping off the top third of the leaves and removing the tougher exterior leaves. Trim bottoms so that they have a flat surface.
3. Add water to the Instant Pot and insert steam rack. Place artichokes upright in a steamer basket and lower basket onto steam rack. Sprinkle artichokes with 1 teaspoon salt. Lock lid.
4. Press the Manual or Pressure Cook button and adjust time to 5 minutes. When timer beeps, quick-release pressure until float valve drops. Unlock lid.
5. Lift artichokes very carefully out of pot (they will be so tender that they may fall apart), transfer to a large plate, and serve with yogurt sauce for dipping.

Steamed Asparagus With Salsa Verde

Servings: 4

Cooking Time: 15 Minutes

Ingredients:

- 1 lb asparagus, trimmed
- 1 tbsp onion, chopped
- Salt and pepper to taste
- 2 tbsp parsley, chopped
- 4 anchovy fillets, chopped
- 2 tbsp extra-virgin olive oil
- 1 tbsp sherry vinegar
- 2 tsp capers, chopped

Directions:

1. Pour 1 cup of water into your Instant Pot and fit in a trivet. Place the asparagus on the trivet. Season with salt and pepper. Seal the lid and cook for 2 minutes on Steam. Once ready, perform a quick pressure release. Add parsley, onion, sherry vinegar, olive oil, anchovies, and capers in a blender and process until everything is well mixed. Drizzle the asparagus with the sauce.

Taco-style Chicken Stew

Servings: 4

Cooking Time: 25 Minutes

Ingredients:

- 2 tbsp butter
- 1 lb chicken breasts
- 1 carrot, chopped
- 1 celery stalk, chopped
- 1 onion, chopped
- 3 garlic cloves, minced
- 3 tbsp Taco Seasoning
- Salt and pepper to taste
- 1 ½ cups diced tomatoes
- 1 lb cubed butternut squash
- 2 cups chicken broth
- 1 tsp lime juice
- 4 lime wedges
- 2 tbsp chopped cilantro

Directions:

1. Melt butter in your Instant Pot on Sauté. Place the celery, onion, carrots, garlic, taco seasoning, black pepper, and salt and cook for 5 minutes, stirring often. Mix in chicken breast, tomatoes, butternut squash, broth, and lime juice. Seal the lid, select Soup and cook for 10 minutes.
2. When done, perform a quick pressure release. Transfer the chicken onto a cutting board and shred it. Put the chicken back in the pot and divide between bowls. Serve topped with cilantro and lime wedges.

Creamy Celery & Green Pea Soup

Servings: 4

Cooking Time: 25 Minutes

Ingredients:

- 3 oz carrots, finely chopped
- 3 oz celery root, chopped
- 1 cup green peas
- 2 tbsp butter
- 2 tbsp parsley, chopped
- 1 egg yolk
- 2 tbsp cream cheese
- Salt and pepper to taste
- 4 cups beef broth

Directions:

1. Add carrots, celery, green peas, butter parsley, egg yolk, cream cheese, salt, pepper, and broth to the Instant Pot and seal the lid. Cook on High Pressure for 10 minutes. When done, release the steam naturally for 10 minutes.

Corn Soup With Chicken & Egg

Servings: 2

Cooking Time: 25 Minutes

Ingredients:

- 1 tbsp cilantro, chopped
- 1 egg
- ½ lb chicken breasts
- 1 leek, chopped
- 1 tbsp sliced shallots
- ¼ tsp nutmeg
- 2 cups water
- ¼ cup corn kernels
- ¼ cup diced carrots
- Salt and pepper to taste

Directions:

1. Slice the chicken breasts into small cubes and place them in your Instant Pot. Add in corn kernels, water, shallots, salt, nutmeg, and black pepper. Seal the lid, select Pressure Cook, and cook for 15 minutes on High.

2. When done, allow a natural release and unlock the lid. Mix in carrots and leek and bring to a boil on Sauté. Beat the egg in a bowl. Once the Soup boil, pour in the beaten egg and toss until well combined and done. Divide between bowls, sprinkle with cilantro, and serve.

Butter-braised Cabbage

Servings: 4

Cooking Time: 30 Minutes

Ingredients:

- 4 tbsp butter
- 1 head cabbage, shredded
- 1 ½ cups vegetable broth
- ½ tsp red pepper flakes
- ½ tsp herbs de Provence
- 1 carrot, grated
- 2 tsp cornstarch

Directions:

1. Melt the butter in your Instant Pot on Sauté. Add in the cabbage and 2-3 tbsp of the vegetable broth and cook for 6 minutes, stirring occasionally. Mix in carrots, herbs de Provence, and the remaining vegetable broth.

2. Seal the lid, select Manual, and cook for 6 minutes on High pressure. When done, perform a quick pressure release and unlock the lid. Remove the cabbage and carrot to a bowl with a slotted spoon.

3. Combine the cornstarch with some of the cooking liquid and pour it into the pot. Press Sauté and cook until the sauce thickens, about 3-4 minutes. Stir in red pepper flakes and pour over the cabbage. Serve warm.

Rosemary Pork Belly Stew

Servings: 6

Cooking Time: 50 Minutes

Ingredients:

- 3 lb sirloin pork roast
- 1 tbsp honey
- 1 tsp chili powder
- 1 tbsp rosemary
- 1 tbsp olive oil
- Salt and pepper to taste

Directions:

1. Combine chili powder, rosemary, salt, and pepper in a bowl and rub them onto the pork. Heat oil on Sauté and sear the pork on all sides. Stir in honey and seal the lid. Cook for 30 minutes on Meat/Stew. Do a natural pressure release for 10 minutes. Carefully unlock the lid.

Mascarpone Mashed Turnips

Servings: 4

Cooking Time: 32 Minutes

Ingredients:

- 1 lb turnips, cubed
- 1 onion, chopped
- ½ tsp ground nutmeg
- ½ cup chicken stock
- Salt and pepper to taste
- ¼ cup sour cream
- 2 tbsp mascarpone

Directions:

1. Place the turnips, onion, and chicken stock in your Instant Pot and seal the lid. Select Manual and cook for 12 minutes on High. Once over, allow a natural release for 10 minutes and unlock the lid. Add in sour cream, nutmeg, and mascarpone and mash it using a potato masher until smooth. Sprinkle with salt and pepper.

Traditional Italian Vegetable Soup

Servings: 6

Cooking Time: 32 Minutes

Ingredients:

- 2 tbsp olive oil
- 1 onion, diced
- 1 cup celery, chopped
- 1 carrot, diced
- 1 green bell pepper, chopped
- 2 cloves garlic, minced
- 3 cups chicken broth
- ½ tsp dried parsley
- ½ tsp dried thyme
- ½ tsp dried oregano
- Salt and pepper to taste
- 2 bay leaves
- 28 oz can diced tomatoes
- 1 tbsp tomato paste
- 2 cups kale
- 14 oz canned navy beans
- ½ cup rice
- ¼ cup Parmesan, shredded

Directions:

1. Warm olive oil on Sauté. Stir in carrot, celery, and onion and cook for 5 minutes until soft. Add garlic and bell pepper and cook for 2 minutes as you stir until aromatic. Stir in pepper, thyme, broth, salt, parsley, oregano, tomatoes, bay leaves, and tomato paste. Mix in rice. Seal the lid and cook on High Pressure for 15 minutes. Do a quick release. Add kale and stir. Use residual heat to slightly wilting the greens. Discard bay leaves. Stir in navy beans and serve topped with Parmesan cheese.

Creamy Bean & Potato Soup

Servings: 4

Cooking Time: 35 Minutes

Ingredients:

- ½ cup canned beans
- 4 cups beef broth
- 1 potato, chopped
- ½ cup heavy cream
- Salt and pepper to taste
- 1 tsp garlic powder

Directions:

1. Add beans, broth, potato, heavy cream, salt, pepper, and garlic powder to the pot, seal the lid, and cook on Manual/Pressure for 10 minutes on High. Release the steam naturally for 10 minutes. Carefully unlock the lid. Transfer the ingredients to a blender. Pulse until smooth. Return the soup to the pot. Press Sauté and add a half cup of water. Cook for 5 more minutes, or until desired thickness. Let it chill for a while before serving.

Mom's Meatball Soup

Servings: 4

Cooking Time: 25 Minutes

Ingredients:

- 2 Yukon Gold potatoes, peeled and diced
- 2 tbsp canola oil
- 1 onion, diced
- 1 garlic clove, minced
- ½ lb ground pork
- 14 oz can diced tomatoes
- 4 cups vegetable broth
- ½ tsp dried oregano
- ½ tsp dried thyme
- Salt and pepper to taste
- 2 tbsp parsley, chopped

Directions:

1. Place the ground pork in a bowl and season with oregano, thyme, salt, and pepper. Mix well with your hands and form form the mixture into small balls.

Warm the canola oil in your Instant Pot on Sauté. Add in the onion and garlic and cook for 3 minutes. Pour in vegetable broth, tomatoes, potatoes, and meatballs and seal the lid. Select Manual and cook for 10 minutes on High pressure. Once ready, perform a quick pressure release and unlock the lid. Sprinkle with par and serve warm.

Mediterranean Meatballs With Mint Sauce

Servings: 4

Cooking Time: 35 Minutes

Ingredients:

- 1 lb lean ground beef
- ¼ cup flour
- 1 tbsp rosemary, chopped
- 1 cup tomato sauce
- 1 large egg, beaten
- ½ tsp salt
- 2 tbsp olive oil
- 1 cup Greek yogurt
- 2 tbsp fresh mint
- 1 garlic clove, crushed

Directions:

1. In a bowl, mix ground beef, rosemary, egg, flour, and salt. Lightly dampen hands and shape into balls. Warm the olive oil in your Instant Pot on Sauté. Fry the balls for 5-6 minutes on all sides. Pour in the tomato sauce and ½ cup of water. Seal the lid and cook on High Pressure for 13 minutes. When ready, do a quick release. Press Sauté and cook until the sauce thickens, about 5 minutes. In a bowl, mix the Greek yogurt, mint, and garlic. Stir well and drizzle over the meatballs. Serve and enjoy!

Beans, Rice, & Grains

Beans, Rice, & Grains

Sausage & Red Bean Stew

Servings: 4

Cooking Time: 50 Minutes

Ingredients:

- 1 cup red beans, soaked
- 4 sausages, sliced
- 6 cups water
- 2 carrots, chopped
- Salt and pepper to taste
- 2 tbsp vegetable oil
- 1 yellow onion, diced
- 1 tomato, chopped
- 2 green onions, chopped
- 2 tbsp cilantro, chopped

Directions:

1. Place red beans and water in your Instant Pot. Seal the lid, select Manual, and cook for 10 minutes on High pressure.Once ready, allow a natural release for 10 minutes and unlock the lid. Drain the beans and set aside. Warm the vegetable oil in the pot on Sauté.
2. Add in sausage, carrots, yellow onion, salt, and pepper and cook for 5 minutes. Stir in tomatoes, green onions, cooked beans, and 1 cup of water. Seal the lid, select Manual, and cook for 15 minutes on High pressure. Once done, perform a quick pressure release and unlock the lid. Scatter with cilantro and serve.

Weeknight Baked Beans

Servings:6

Cooking Time: 8 Minutes

Ingredients:

- 2 teaspoons olive oil
- 2 slices bacon, diced
- 1 can great northern beans, drained and rinsed
- 1 can pinto beans, drained and rinsed
- 1 teaspoon salt
- ¼ teaspoon ground black pepper
- ½ cup molasses barbecue sauce
- 1 tablespoon yellow mustard
- 1 cup water

Directions:

1. Line a plate with paper towels.
2. Press the Sauté button on the Instant Pot and heat oil. Add bacon. Stir-fry 3–5 minutes until bacon is almost crisp. Transfer bacon to prepared plate to absorb grease. Press the Cancel button. Rinse pot.
3. In a 7-cup glass baking dish, add bacon, beans, salt, pepper, barbecue sauce, and mustard.
4. Add water to the Instant Pot and insert steam rack. Place glass baking dish on top of steam rack. Lock lid.
5. Press the Manual or Pressure Cook button and adjust time to 3 minutes. When timer beeps, quick-release pressure until float valve drops. Unlock lid.
6. Transfer beans to a bowl. Serve warm.

Risotto With Broccoli & Grana Padano

Servings: 6

Cooking Time: 35 Minutes

Ingredients:

- 2 tbsp Grana Padano cheese flakes
- 10 oz broccoli florets
- 1 onion, chopped
- 3 tbsp butter
- 2 cups carnaroli rice, rinsed
- ¼ cup dry white wine
- 4 cups chicken stock
- Salt and pepper to taste
- 2 tbsp Grana Padano, grated

Directions:

1. Warm butter on Sauté. Stir-fry onion for 3 minutes until translucent. Add in broccoli and rice and cook for 5 minutes, stirring occasionally. Pour wine into the pot and scrape away any browned bits of food from the pan.
2. Stir in stock, pepper, and salt. Seal the lid, press Manual and cook on High for 15 minutes. Release the pressure quickly. Sprinkle with grated Grana Padano cheese and stir well. Top with flaked Grana Padano cheese to serve.

Risotto With Spring Vegetables & Shrimp

Servings: 4

Cooking Time: 40 Minutes

Ingredients:

- 1 tbsp avocado oil
- 1 lb asparagus, chopped
- 1 cup spinach, chopped
- 1 cup mushrooms, sliced
- 1 cup rice
- 1 ¼ cups chicken broth
- ¾ cup coconut milk
- 1 tbsp coconut oil
- 1 lb shrimp, deveined
- Salt and pepper to taste
- ¾ cup Parmesan, shredded

Directions:

1. Warm the avocado oil on Sauté. Add spinach, mushrooms, and asparagus and sauté for 5 minutes until cooked through. Add in rice, coconut milk, and chicken broth as you stir. Seal the lid, press Manual, and cook for 20 minutes on High Pressure.
2. Do a quick release. Place the rice on a serving plate. Press Sauté. Heat the coconut oil. Add shrimp and cook for 6 minutes until it turns pink. Set the shrimp over rice and season with pepper and salt. Serve topped with Parmesan cheese.

Bean & Potato Hash

Servings: 4

Cooking Time: 15 Minutes

Ingredients:

- 2 cups peeled, chopped sweet potatoes
- 1 cup canned cannellini beans
- 2 tbsp olive oil
- 1 onion, chopped
- 1 clove garlic, minced
- 2 tsp hot chili powder
- 1 cup veggie broth
- ¼ cup chives, chopped

Directions:

1. Warm olive oil in your Instant Pot on Sauté. Place in onion and cook for 2-3 minutes. Add in garlic and cook until fragrant. Stir in sweet potatoes and chili powder and toss to coat. Mix in veggie broth. Seal the lid, select Manual, and cook for 3 minutes on High. Once over, perform a quick pressure release and unlock the lid. Stir in cannellini beans. Serve topped with chives.

Butter Beans With Pesto

Servings: 4

Cooking Time: 40 Minutes

Ingredients:

- 1 cup butter beans, soaked
- 3 cups chicken stock
- 1 tsp thyme
- Salt and pepper to taste
- ½ cup heavy cream
- ½ cup basil pesto

Directions:

1. Place butter beans, chicken stock, thyme, pepper, and salt in your Instant Pot. Seal the lid, select Manual, and cook for 25 minutes on High. Once ready, perform a quick pressure release; unlock the lid. Stir in heavy cream and simmer for 5 minutes on Sauté. Serve topped with pesto.

Easy Couscous

Servings:6

Cooking Time: 4 Minutes

Ingredients:

- 2 cups couscous
- 2½ cups water
- 1 cup chicken broth
- 1 teaspoon sea salt
- 1 tablespoon butter
- 1 teaspoon lemon zest

Directions:

1. Place all ingredients into the Instant Pot. Lock lid.
2. Press the Manual button and adjust time to 4 minutes. When timer beeps, let pressure release naturally until float valve drops and then unlock lid. Serve.

Bell Pepper & Pinto Bean Stew

Servings: 6

Cooking Time: 55 Minutes

Ingredients:

- 2 tbsp olive oil
- 1 onion, chopped
- 1 red bell pepper, chopped
- 1 tbsp dried oregano
- 1 tbsp ground cumin
- 1 tsp red pepper flakes
- 3 cups vegetable stock
- 2 cups pinto beans, soaked
- 14 oz can tomatoes, diced
- 1 tbsp white wine vinegar
- ½ cup chives, chopped
- ¼ cup fresh corn kernels

Directions:

1. Set to Sauté your Instant Pot and heat oil. Stir in bell pepper, pepper flakes, oregano, onion, and cumin. Cook for 3 minutes. Mix in pinto beans, stock, and tomatoes. Seal the lid, select Manual, and cook for 30 minutes on High Pressure. Release the pressure naturally for 10 minutes. Add in vinegar. Divide among serving plates and top with corn and fresh chives to serve.

Instant Pot
Cookbook

Creamy Chicken And Broccoli Over Rice

Servings: 8

Cooking Time: 45 Minutes

Ingredients:

- ¼ cup flour
- 2 teaspoons salt
- ½ teaspoon ground black pepper
- 1 tablespoon Italian seasoning
- 1 pound chicken thighs, cut in 1" chunks
- 1 tablespoon olive oil
- 1 large onion, peeled and diced
- 2 cups wild rice, rinsed
- 3 cups vegetable broth
- 1½ cups water
- 2 cups steamed broccoli florets
- ¼ cup heavy cream
- ¼ cup grated Parmesan cheese

Directions:

1. In a small bowl, combine flour, salt, pepper, and Italian seasoning. Add chicken to seasoning mix and toss to coat. Set aside.
2. Press the Sauté button on the Instant Pot and heat oil. Cook onions for 3–5 minutes until translucent. Add rice and toss to combine.
3. Add chicken in an even layer over ingredients in Instant Pot. Gently pour in broth and water. Lock lid.
4. Press the Multigrain button. When the timer beeps, let pressure release naturally for 10 minutes. Quick-release any additional pressure until float valve drops and then unlock lid. Add broccoli. Stir. Add cream and Parmesan cheese. Stir. Allow mixture to thicken unlidded in Instant Pot for 5 minutes.
5. Transfer to a serving dish and serve warm.

Provençal Rice

Servings: 6

Cooking Time: 45 Minutes

Ingredients:

- 2 tbsp butter
- 1 onion, diced
- 2 garlic cloves, minced
- 2 cups brown rice
- 3 cups vegetable stock
- 1 tsp herbs de Provence
- 3 anchovy fillets, finely chopped
- 6 pitted Kalamata olives

Directions:

1. Melt butter in your Instant Pot on Sauté and add in onion and garlic; cook for 3 minutes. Stir in rice and herbs for 1 minute and pour in the stock. Seal the lid, select Manual, and cook for 22 minutes on High. When ready, allow a natural release for 10 minutes and unlock the lid. Stir in anchovy fillets. Serve topped with Kalamata olives.

Honey Oat & Pumpkin Granola

Servings: 4

Cooking Time: 45 Minutes

Ingredients:

- 1 tbsp soft butter
- 1 cup steel-cut oats
- 1 cup pumpkin puree
- 3 cups water
- 2 tsp cinnamon
- A pinch of salt
- ¼ cup clear honey
- 1 tsp pumpkin pie spice

Directions:

1. Set your Instant Pot to Sauté and melt in the butter. Stir in oats and cook for 3 minutes. Add in pumpkin puree, water, cinnamon, salt, honey, and pumpkin spice and stir. Seal the lid, select Manual, and cook for 10 minutes on High. Once ready, allow a natural release for 10 minutes. Stir the granola and let sit for 10 minutes. Serve.

Ziti Green Minestrone

Servings: 4

Cooking Time: 25 Minutes

Ingredients:

- ¼ cup grated Pecorino Romano
- 3 tbsp olive oil
- 1 onion, diced
- 1 celery stalk, diced
- 1 large carrot, diced
- 14 oz can diced tomatoes
- 4 oz ziti pasta
- 1 cup chopped zucchini
- 1 bay leaf
- 1 tbsp mixed herbs
- ¼ tbsp cayenne pepper
- Salt and pepper to taste
- 1 garlic clove, minced
- 1/3 cup olive pesto pasta

Directions:

1. Heat olive oil on Sauté. Cook onion, celery, garlic, and carrot for 3 minutes, stirring occasionally until the vegetables are softened. Stir in ziti, tomatoes, 3 cups water, zucchini, bay leaf, mixed herbs, cayenne, pepper, and salt. Seal the lid and cook on High for 4 minutes.
2. Do a natural pressure release for 10 minutes. Adjust the taste and remove the bay leaf. Ladle the soup into bowls and drizzle the pesto over. Serve topped with Pecorino cheese.

Chicken & Broccoli Fettuccine Alfredo

Servings: 2

Cooking Time: 15 Minutes

Ingredients:

- 1 cup cooked chicken breasts, chopped
- 1 cup broccoli florets
- 8 oz fettuccine, halved
- 1 tsp chicken seasoning
- 1 jar Alfredo sauce
- Salt and pepper to taste
- 1 tbsp parsley, chopped
- 1 tbsp Parmesan, grated

Directions:

1. Add 2 cups of water, fettuccine, and chicken seasoning to your Instant Pot. Place a steamer basket on top and add in the broccoli. Seal the lid, select Manual, and cook for 3 minutes on High. Once over, perform a quick pressure release. Drain the pasta and set aside. In a bowl, place Alfredo sauce, broccoli, parsley, and cooked chicken. Add in the pasta and mix to combine. Season with salt and pepper. Serve topped with Parmesan cheese.

Millet Tabouleh

Servings:4

Cooking Time: 10 Minutes

Ingredients:

- 1½ cups chopped fresh parsley
- ¼ cup chopped fresh mint leaves
- 1 cup peeled and diced red onion
- ¼ cup small-diced zucchini
- ½ cup peeled, seeded, and small-diced cucumber
- 4 small Roma tomatoes, seeded and diced
- ¼ cup plus 2 teaspoons olive oil, divided
- ¼ cup lemon juice
- 1 teaspoon lemon zest
- 1½ teaspoons sea salt, divided
- ¼ teaspoon ground black pepper
- 1 cup millet
- 2 cups vegetable broth

Directions:

1. In a medium bowl, combine parsley, mint, onion, zucchini, cucumber, tomatoes, ¼ cup olive oil, lemon juice, lemon zest, 1 teaspoon salt, and pepper. Cover and refrigerate for 30 minutes up to overnight.
2. Drizzle 2 teaspoons olive oil in Instant Pot. Add millet to Instant Pot in an even layer. Add broth and remaining ½ teaspoon salt. Lock lid.
3. Press the Rice button. When the timer beeps, let pressure release naturally for 5 minutes. Quick-release any additional pressure until float valve drops and then unlock lid.
4. Transfer millet to a serving bowl and set aside to cool. When cooled, add to refrigerated mixture and stir. Serve.

Spinach & Cheese Filled Conchiglie Shells

Servings: 6

Cooking Time: 45 Minutes

Ingredients:

- ¾ cup grated Pecorino Romano cheese
- 2 cups onions, chopped
- 1 cup carrots, chopped
- 3 garlic cloves, minced
- 3 ½ tbsp olive oil
- 28-oz can tomatoes, diced
- 12 oz conchiglie pasta
- 1 tbsp olive oil for greasing
- 2 cups ricotta, crumbled
- 1 ½ cups feta, crumbled
- 2 cups spinach, chopped
- 2 tbsp chopped fresh chives
- 1 tbsp chopped fresh dill
- Salt and pepper to taste
- 1 cup shredded cheddar

Directions:

1. Warm olive oil on Sauté. Add in onions, carrots, and garlic and cook for 5 minutes until tender. Stir in tomatoes and cook for another 10 minutes. Remove to a bowl. Wipe the pot with a damp cloth, add pasta, and cover with enough water. Seal the lid and cook for 5 minutes on High Pressure. Do a quick release and drain the pasta. Lightly grease olive oil on a baking sheet.
2. In a bowl, combine feta and ricotta cheese. Add in spinach, Pecorino Romano cheese, dill, chives, salt, and pepper and stir. Using a spoon, fill the conchiglie shells with the mixture. Spread 4 cups of the tomato sauce on a baking sheet. Place the stuffed shells over with seam-sides down and sprinkle cheddar cheese on the top. Cover with aluminum foil.
3. Pour 1 cup of water into the cooker and insert a trivet. Lower the baking dish onto the trivet. Seal the lid and cook for 15 minutes on High Pressure. Do a quick release. Take away the foil. Top with the remaining tomato sauce before serving.

Hawaiian Rice

Servings: 4

Cooking Time: 30 Minutes

Ingredients:

- 2 tsp olive oil
- 1 ½ cups coconut water
- 1 cup jasmine rice
- 2 green onions, sliced
- ½ pineapple, and chopped
- Salt to taste
- ¼ tsp red pepper flakes

Directions:

1. Stir olive oil, water, rice, pineapple, and salt in your Instant Pot. Seal the lid, select Manual, and cook for 10 minutes on low pressure. Once over, allow a natural release for 10 minutes, then a quick pressure release. Carefully unlock the lid. Using a fork, fluff the rice. Scatter with green onions and red pepper flakes and serve.

Wild Rice Pilaf

Servings: 4

Cooking Time: 20 Minutes

Ingredients:

- 1 cup wild rice
- 2 tbsp butter
- Salt and pepper to taste
- 2 tbsp chives, chopped

Directions:

1. Stir the rice, butter, 2 cups of water, salt, and pepper in your Instant Pot. Seal the lid, select Manual, and cook for 5 minutes on High pressure. When ready, allow a natural release for 10 minutes and unlock the lid. Using a fork, fluff the rice. Top with chives and serve.

Vegan & Vegetarian

Vegan & Vegetarian

Two-cheese Carrot Sauce

Servings: 4

Cooking Time: 25 Minutes

Ingredients:

- 1 carrot, shredded
- 1 cup cream cheese
- ½ cup Gorgonzola cheese
- 3 cups vegetable broth
- 1 cup Gruyere, crumbled
- Salt and pepper to taste
- 1 tsp garlic powder
- 1 tbsp parsley, chopped

Directions:

1. Combine carrot, cream cheese, gorgonzola cheese, broth, gruyere, salt, pepper, garlic powder, and parsley in a large bowl. Pour in the Instant Pot, seal the lid and cook on High Pressure for 8 minutes. Do a natural release for 10 minutes. Store for up to 5 days.

Corn & Lentil Hummus With Parmesan

Servings: 6

Cooking Time: 45 Minutes

Ingredients:

- 1 lb lentils, cooked
- 1 cup sweet corn
- 2 tomatoes, diced
- 3 tbsp tomato paste
- ½ tbsp dried oregano
- 2 tbsp Parmesan cheese
- 1 tbsp salt
- ½ tbsp red pepper flakes
- 3 tbsp olive oil
- ¼ cup red wine

Directions:

1. Heat olive oil on Sauté and add tomatoes, tomato paste, and ½ cup of water. Sprinkle with salt, pepper flakes, and oregano and stir-fry for 5 minutes. Add lentils, sweet corn, and red wine. Pour in ½ cup of water and seal the lid. Cook on High Pressure for 2 minutes. Do a quick release. Set aside to cool completely and refrigerate for 30 minutes. Sprinkle with Parmesan cheese before serving.

Parmesan Topped Vegetable Mash

Servings: 6

Cooking Time: 15 Minutes

Ingredients:

- 3 lb Yukon gold potatoes, chopped
- 2 cups cauliflower florets
- 1 carrot, chopped
- 1 cup Parmesan, shredded
- ¼ cup butter, melted
- ¼ cup milk
- 1 tsp salt
- 1 garlic clove, minced
- 2 tbsp parsley, chopped

Directions:

1. Into the pot, add potatoes, cauliflower, carrot and salt; cover with enough water. Seal the lid and cook on High Pressure for 10 minutes. Release the pressure quickly. Drain the vegetables and mash them with a potato masher. Add garlic, butter, and milk. Whisk until well incorporated. Top with Parmesan cheese and parsley.

Roman Stewed Beans With Tomatoes

Servings: 6

Cooking Time: 30 Minutes

Ingredients:

- 2 cups cranberry beans
- 2 onions, chopped
- 3 carrots, chopped
- 3 tomatoes, peeled, diced
- 3 tbsp olive oil
- 2 tbsp parsley, chopped
- 2 cups water
- Salt and pepper to taste

Directions:

1. Heat olive oil on Sauté, and stir-fry the onions for 3-4 minutes until translucent. Add in carrots and tomatoes. Stir well and cook for 5 minutes. Stir in beans, salt, black pepper and water, and seal the lid. Cook on High Pressure for 15 minutes. Do a quick release and serve hot sprinkled with fresh parsley.

Traditional Italian Pesto

Servings: 4

Cooking Time: 20 Minutes

Ingredients:

- 3 zucchini, peeled, chopped
- 1 eggplant, peeled, chopped
- 3 red bell peppers, chopped
- ½ cup basil-tomato juice
- ½ tbsp salt
- 2 tbsp olive oil

Directions:

1. Add zucchini, eggplant, bell peppers, basil-tomato juice, salt, and olive oil to the pot and give it a good stir. Pour 1 cup of water. Seal the lid and cook on High Pressure for 15 minutes. Do a quick release. Set aside to cool completely. Serve as a cold salad or a side dish.

Coconut Milk Yogurt With Honey

Servings: 6

Cooking Time: 15 Hours

Ingredients:

- 2 cans coconut milk
- 1 tbsp gelatin
- 1 tbsp honey
- 1 tbsp probiotic powder
- Zest from 1 lime

Directions:

1. Into the pot, stir in gelatin and coconut milk until well dissolved. Seal the lid, Press Yogurt until the display is reading "Boil". Once done, the screen will then display "Yogurt". Ensure milk temperature is at 180°F. Remove steel pot from Pressure cooker base and place into a large ice bath to cool milk for 5 minutes to reach 112°F.
2. Remove the pot from the ice bath and wipe the outside dry. Into the coconut milk mixture, add probiotic powder, honey, and Lime zest, and stir to combine. Return steel pot to the base of the Instant Pot. Seal the lid, press Yogurt, and cook for 10 hours. Once complete, spoon yogurt into glass jars with rings and lids; place

in the refrigerator to chill for 4 hours to thicken.

Mashed Potato Balls With Tomato Sauce

Servings: 4

Cooking Time: 55 Minutes

Ingredients:

- 2 potatoes, peeled
- 1 onion, peeled, chopped
- 1 lb spinach, torn
- ¼ cup mozzarella, shredded
- 2 eggs, beaten
- Salt and pepper to taste
- 1 tsp dried oregano
- 1 cup whole milk
- ¼ cup flour
- ¼ cup cornflour
- 2 garlic cloves
- Tomato sauce:
- 1 lb tomatoes, chopped
- 1 onion, chopped
- 2 garlic cloves, minced
- 3 tsp olive oil
- ¼ cup white wine
- 1 tsp sugar
- 1 tsp dried rosemary
- ½ tsp salt
- 1 tsp tomato paste

Directions:

1. Place the potatoes in your Instant Pot and add enough water to cover. Seal the lid and cook on High Pressure for 13 minutes. Do a quick release. Add 1 cup of milk and mash with a potato masher. Whisk in eggs, add onion, spinach, mozzarella, salt, pepper, oregano, flour, cornflour, and garlic, and mix with hands. Shape into balls and set aside. Press Sauté, warm olive oil, and stir-fry onion and garlic until translucent.
2. Stir in tomatoes and cook until tender, about 10 minutes. Pour in the wine and add sugar, rosemary, and salt. Stir in 1 tsp of tomato paste and mix well. Cook for five more minutes. Place the potato balls in the cooker and seal with the lid. Cook on High Pressure for 5 minutes. Do a natural release for 10 minutes. Ser

Stuffed Bell Peppers

Servings:4

Cooking Time: 15 Minutes

Ingredients:

- 4 large bell peppers
- 2 cups cooked white rice
- 1 medium onion, peeled and diced
- 3 small Roma tomatoes, diced
- ¼ cup marinara sauce
- 1 cup corn kernels (cut from the cob is preferred)
- ¼ cup sliced black olives
- ¼ cup canned cannellini beans, rinsed and drained
- ¼ cup canned black beans, rinsed and drained
- 1 teaspoon sea salt
- 1 teaspoon garlic powder
- ½ cup vegetable broth
- 2 tablespoons grated Parmesan cheese

Directions:

1. Cut off the bell pepper tops as close to the tops as possible. Hollow out and discard seeds. Poke a few small holes in the bottom of the peppers to allow drippings to drain.
2. In a medium bowl, combine remaining ingredients except for broth and Parmesan cheese. Stuff equal amounts of mixture into each of the bell peppers.
3. Place trivet into the Instant Pot and pour in the broth. Set the peppers upright on the trivet. Lock lid.
4. Press the Manual button and adjust time to 15 minutes. When timer beeps, let pressure release naturally until float valve drops and then unlock lid.
5. Serve immediately and garnish with Parmesan cheese.

Millet Eggplant Pilaf

Servings:4

Cooking Time: 17 Minutes

Ingredients:

- 1 tablespoon butter
- ¼ cup peeled and diced onion
- 1 cup peeled and diced eggplant
- 1 small Roma tomato, seeded and diced
- 1 cup millet
- 2 cups vegetable broth
- 1 teaspoon sea salt
- ¼ teaspoon ground black pepper
- ⅛ teaspoon saffron
- ⅛ teaspoon cayenne pepper
- 1 tablespoon chopped fresh chives

Directions:

1. Press Sauté button on Instant Pot. Add butter and melt. Add onion and cook 3–5 minutes until translucent. Toss in eggplant and stir-fry for 2 more minutes. Add diced tomato.
2. Add millet to Instant Pot in an even layer. Gently pour in broth. Lock lid.
3. Press the Rice button. When timer beeps, let pressure release naturally for 5 minutes. Quick-release any additional pressure until float valve drops and then unlock lid.
4. Transfer pot ingredients to a serving bowl. Season with salt, pepper, saffron, and cayenne pepper. Garnish with chives.

Carrot & Chickpea Boil With Tomatoes

Servings: 4

Cooking Time: 25 Minutes

Ingredients:

- ½ cup button mushrooms, chopped
- 1 cup canned chickpeas
- 1 onion, peeled, chopped
- 1 lb string beans, trimmed
- 1 apple, cubed
- ½ cup raisins
- 2 carrots, chopped
- 2 garlic cloves, crushed
- 4 cherry tomatoes
- 1 tbsp grated ginger
- ½ cup orange juice

Directions:

1. Place mushrooms, chickpeas, onion, beans, apple, raisins, carrots, garlic, cherry tomatoes, ginger, and orange juice in the Instant Pot. Pour enough water to cover. Cook on High Pressure for 8 minutes. Do a natural release for 10 minutes. Serve warm.

Cali Dogs

Servings:4

Cooking Time: 0 Minutes

Ingredients:

- 2 cups water
- 8 meat-free, plant-based hot dogs
- 8 hot dog buns
- ½ cup alfalfa sprouts
- 1 medium avocado, peeled, pitted, and diced
- ½ cup crumbled goat cheese

Directions:

1. Pour water into the Instant Pot. Add hot dogs. Lock lid.
2. Press the Manual or Pressure Cook button and adjust time to 0 minutes. When timer beeps, quick-release pressure until float valve drops. Unlock lid.
3. Assemble hot dogs by placing them in buns and topping with remaining ingredients. Serve warm.

Green Bean Salad With Cheese & Nuts

Servings: 6

Cooking Time: 15 Minutes

Ingredients:

- Juice from 1 lemon
- 2 lb green beans, trimmed
- 1 cup toasted pine nuts
- 1 cup feta, crumbled
- 6 tbsp olive oil
- Salt and pepper to taste

Directions:

1. Add water and set rack over the water and the steamer basket on the rack. Loosely heap green beans into the steamer basket. Seal lid and cook on High Pressure for 5 minutes. Release pressure quickly. Drop green beans into a salad bowl. Top with olive oil, feta cheese, salt, lemon juice, black pepper, and pine nuts.

Carrot & Sweet Potato Thick Soup

Servings: 4

Cooking Time: 40 Minutes

Ingredients:

- 4 sweet potatoes, cut into bite-sized pieces
- 2 carrots, chopped
- 1 onion, chopped
- 6 tbsp olive oil
- 2 tbsp tomato sauce
- 1 tbsp celery, chopped
- 1 tbsp parsley, chopped
- Salt and pepper to taste

Directions:

1. Heat olive oil on Sauté. Add onion, carrots, celery, and potatoes. Stir-fry for 2 minutes. Stir in 4 cups of water and tomato sauce. Seal the lid and cook for 25 minutes on High Pressure. Do a quick release. Open the pot and add celery, parsley, salt, and pepper. Seal again, and cook for 5 minutes on High. Do a quick release.

Saucy Millet And Corn

Servings:4

Cooking Time: 10 Minutes

Ingredients:

- 2 teaspoons olive oil
- 1 cup millet
- 2 cups vegetable broth
- 1 teaspoon sea salt
- 1 can corn kernels
- 1 can tomato sauce
- ¼ cup grated Gruyère cheese

Directions:

1. Drizzle 2 teaspoons olive oil in Instant Pot. Layer millet into pot. Add vegetable broth and salt. Lock lid.
2. Press the Rice button. When timer beeps, let pressure release naturally for 5 minutes. Quick-release any additional pressure until float valve drops and then unlock lid.
3. Transfer millet to a serving bowl. Toss corn, tomato sauce, and Gruyère cheese in millet. Serve warm.

English Vegetable Potage

Servings: 4

Cooking Time: 50 Minutes

Ingredients:

- 1 lb potatoes, cut into bite-sized pieces
- 2 carrots, peeled, chopped
- 3 celery stalks, chopped
- 2 onions, peeled, chopped
- 1 zucchini, sliced
- A handful of celery leaves
- 2 tbsp butter, unsalted
- 3 tbsp olive oil
- 2 cups vegetable broth
- 1 tbsp paprika
- Salt and pepper to taste
- 2 bay leaves

Directions:

1. Warm olive oil on Sauté and stir-fry the onions for 3-4 minutes until translucent. Add carrots, celery, zucchini, and ¼ cup of broth. Continue to cook for 10 more minutes, stirring constantly. Stir in potatoes, paprika, salt, pepper, bay leaves, remaining broth, and celery leaves. Seal the lid and cook on Meat/Stew for 30 minutes on High. Do a quick release and stir in butter.

Blood Orange And Goat Cheese Wheat Berry Salad

Servings:6

Cooking Time: 35 Minutes

Ingredients:

- 3 tablespoons olive oil, divided
- 1 cup wheat berries
- 2 cups water
- ½ cup dried cranberries
- Juice and zest of ½ medium blood orange
- 1 tablespoon balsamic vinegar
- ½ teaspoon salt
- ¼ cup crumbled goat cheese

Directions:

1. Press Sauté button on Instant Pot and heat 1 table-

spoon oil. Add wheat berries. Stir-fry 4–5 minutes until browned and fragrant. Add water. Press the Cancel button. Lock lid.

2. Press the Manual or Pressure Cook button and adjust time to 30 minutes. When timer beeps, let pressure release naturally for 10 minutes. Quick-release any additional pressure until float valve drops. Unlock lid.
3. Let cool 10 minutes and drain any additional liquid.
4. Transfer cooled berries to a medium bowl and add remaining ingredients, including remaining oil. Refrigerate covered. Serve chilled.

Quick Cassoulet

Servings:6

Cooking Time: 45 Minutes

Ingredients:

- 1 tablespoon olive oil
- 1 medium yellow onion, peeled and diced
- 2 cups dried cannellini beans, rinsed and drained
- 2 medium carrots, peeled and diced small
- 1 tablespoon Italian seasoning
- 1 teaspoon garlic salt
- ½ teaspoon ground black pepper
- 2 ½ cups vegetable broth
- 1 can diced tomatoes, including juice
- 4 vegan smoked apple sausages, each cut into 4 sections

Directions:

1. Press the Sauté button on the Instant Pot and heat oil. Add onion and stir-fry 3–5 minutes until onions are translucent. Add beans and toss.
2. Add carrots, Italian seasoning, garlic salt, and pepper.
3. Gently pour in broth and diced tomatoes. Press the Cancel button. Lock lid.
4. Press the Bean button and cook for the default time of 30 minutes. When timer beeps, let pressure release naturally for 10 minutes. Quick-release any additional pressure until float valve drops. Press the Cancel button. Unlock lid. Add sausage.
5. Press the Sauté button on the Instant Pot, press the Adjust button to change the temperature to Less, and simmer bean mixture unlidded 10 minutes to thicken. Transfer to a serving bowl and carefully toss. Serve warm.

Poultry

Poultry

Spring Onion Buffalo Wings

Servings: 6

Cooking Time: 30 Minutes

Ingredients:

- 2 lb chicken wings, sectioned
- 2 spring onions, sliced diagonally
- ½ cup hot pepper sauce
- 1 tbsp Worcestershire sauce
- 3 tbsp butter
- Sea salt to taste
- 2 tbsp sugar, light brown

Directions:

1. Combine hot sauce, Worcestershire sauce, butter, salt, and brown sugar in a bowl and microwave for 20 seconds until the butter melts. Pour 1 cup of water into your Instant Pot and fit in a trivet. Place the chicken wings on the trivet and seal the lid. Select Manual and cook for 10 minutes on High pressure.
2. Once done, perform a quick pressure release and unlock the lid. Remove chicken wings to a baking dish and brush the top with marinade. Broil for 4-5 minutes, turn the wings and brush more marinade. Broil for 4-5 minutes more. Top with spring onions and serve.

Harissa Chicken Thighs

Servings: 4

Cooking Time: 25 Minutes

Ingredients:

- 2 lb boneless chicken thighs
- 2 tbsp harissa
- ¼ cup soy sauce
- 1 tbsp ketchup
- 2 tbsp olive oil
- ¼ cup honey
- 2 tsp garlic powder
- 2 cups cooked rice
- Salt and pepper to taste

Directions:

1. Place soy sauce, ketchup, olive oil, honey, garlic powder, harissa, pepper, and salt in your Instant Pot and stir. Add in chicken thighs and pour in 1 cup of water. Seal the lid, select Manual, and cook for 20 minutes on High pressure.Once done, perform a quick pressure release and unlock the lid. Serve with a bed of rice.

Creamy Mascarpone Chicken

Servings: 4

Cooking Time: 30 Minutes

Ingredients:

- 8 bacon slices, cooked and crumbled
- 1 lb chicken breasts
- 8 oz mascarpone cheese
- 1 tbsp Dijon mustard
- 1 tsp ranch seasoning
- 3 tbsp cornstarch
- ½ cup cheddar, shredded

Directions:

1. Place the chicken breasts, mustard, and mascarpone cheese in your Instant Pot. Add in ranch seasoning and 1 cup of water. Seal the lid, select Manual, and cook for 15 minutes on High pressure. Once ready, perform a quick pressure release and unlock the lid. Remove the chicken and shred it. Add in cornstarch, shredded chicken, cheese, and bacon and cook for 3 minutes on Sauté. Lock the lid and let chill for a few minutes. Serve.

Bbq Shredded Chicken Sandwiches

Servings:6

Cooking Time: 15 Minutes

Ingredients:

- 1 cup chicken broth
- 2 pounds boneless, skinless chicken breasts
- 2 cups barbecue sauce
- 1 small sweet onion, peeled and grated
- 6 hamburger buns
- 24 dill pickle slices

Directions:

1. Add broth, chicken breasts, barbecue sauce, and onion to the Instant Pot. Lock lid.
2. Press the Manual or Pressure Cook button and adjust time to 15 minutes. When timer beeps, let pressure release naturally for 10 minutes. Quick-release any additional pressure until float valve drops. Unlock lid. Check chicken using a meat thermometer to ensure internal temperature is at least 165°F.
3. Using two forks, pull apart chicken in pot. Using a slotted spoon, transfer chicken to hamburger buns and place 4 pickle slices on each. Serve warm.

Tasty Indian Chicken Curry

Servings: 6

Cooking Time: 30 Minutes

Ingredients:

- 1 can coconut milk, refrigerated overnight
- 2 lb boneless, skinless chicken legs
- 2 tbsp butter
- 1 large onion, minced
- 1 tbsp grated fresh ginger
- 1 tbsp minced fresh garlic
- ½ tsp ground turmeric
- 1 tbsp Kashmiri chili powder
- 3 tomatoes, pureed
- 2 tbsp Indian curry paste
- 2 tbsp dried fenugreek
- 1 tsp garam masala
- Salt to taste

Directions:

1. Melt butter on Sauté in your Instant Pot. Add in onion and cook for 3 minutes until fragrant. Stir in ginger, turmeric, garlic, and red chili powder for 2 minutes. Place the water from the coconut milk can in a bowl and mix with pureed tomatoes and chicken. Pour in the onion mixture.
2. Seal the lid and cook on High Pressure for 8 minutes. Release the pressure quickly. Stir in coconut milk, fenugreek, salt, curry paste, and garam masala. Simmer for 10 minutes until the sauce thickens on Sauté. Serve.

Mediterranean Duck With Olives

Servings: 4

Cooking Time: 20 Minutes

Ingredients:

- ½ cup sun-dried tomatoes, chopped
- 1 lb duck breasts, halved
- 2 tbsp olive oil
- ½ tbsp Italian seasoning
- Salt and pepper to taste
- 2 garlic cloves, minced
- ½ cup chicken stock
- ¾ cup heavy cream
- 1 cup kale, chopped
- ½ cup Parmesan, grated
- 10 Kalamata olives, pitted

Directions:

1. Combine olive oil, Italian seasoning, pepper, salt, and garlic in a bowl. Add in the duck breasts and toss to coat. Set your Instant Pot to Sauté. Place in duck breasts and cook for 5-6 minutes on both sides. Pour in chicken stock and seal the lid. Select Manual and cook for 4 minutes.
2. When done, perform a quick pressure release and unlock the lid. Mix in heavy cream, tomatoes, Kalamata olives, and kale and cook for 5 minutes on Sauté. Serve topped with Parmesan cheese.

Famous Chicken Adobo

Servings: 4

Cooking Time: 50 Minutes

Ingredients:

- 4 chicken thighs
- Salt and pepper to taste
- 2 tbsp olive oil
- ¼ cup white vinegar
- ¼ cup soy sauce
- 1 tbsp honey
- 1 onion, chopped
- 2 garlic cloves, crushed
- 2 bay leaves
- 2 tbsp cilantro, chopped

Directions:

1. Warm the olive oil in your Instant Pot on Sauté. Sprinkle chicken with salt and pepper. Place it in the pot and brown for 8 minutes on all sides. Stir in vinegar, soy sauce, honey, onion, garlic, bay leaves, 1 cup of water, and pepper. Seal the lid, select Manual, and cook for 20 minutes on High pressure.
2. Once done, perform a quick pressure release and unlock the lid. Simmer for 10 minutes on Sauté until the sauce thickens. Discard bay leaves and top with cilantro. Serve.

Bbq Chicken Legs

Servings:5

Cooking Time: 15 Minutes

Ingredients:

- 1 cup chicken broth
- 3 pounds chicken legs/drumsticks
- ¾ cup barbecue sauce

Directions:

1. Insert trivet into Instant Pot. Add chicken broth. Arrange chicken standing up, meaty-side down, on the trivet. Lock lid.
2. Press the Poultry button and cook for the default time of 15 minutes. When timer beeps, let pressure release naturally for 10 minutes. Quick-release any additional pressure until float valve drops and then unlock lid. Check the chicken using a meat thermometer to ensure the internal temperature is at least 165°F.
3. Remove chicken from pot. In a large bowl, gently toss chicken legs in the barbecue sauce and serve.

Lemongrass Chicken

Servings:8

Cooking Time: 10 Minutes

Ingredients:

- 1 tablespoon fish sauce
- 1 tablespoon soy sauce
- ⅛ cup freshly squeezed lime juice
- 1 tablespoon honey
- ½ teaspoon sea salt
- ¼ teaspoon ground turmeric
- ⅛ teaspoon red pepper flakes
- ¼ cup minced lemongrass, tough layers removed
- 3 pounds boneless, skinless chicken thighs
- 1 cup chicken broth
- ¼ cup chopped fresh cilantro

Directions:

1. In a large bowl, whisk together fish sauce, soy sauce, lime juice, honey, salt, turmeric, red pepper flakes, and lemongrass. Toss chicken in sauce and refrigerate covered for 1 hour.

2. Place trivet in Instant Pot. Pour in chicken broth. Arrange chicken on a steamer basket and lower onto the trivet. Lock lid.
3. Press the Manual button and adjust time to 10 minutes. When timer beeps, let pressure release naturally for 10 minutes. Quick-release any additional pressure until the float valve drops and then unlock lid. Check the chicken using a meat thermometer to ensure the internal temperature is at least 165°F.
4. Using a slotted spoon, transfer chicken to a serving tray. Garnish with chopped cilantro.

Pickleback Wings

Servings:6

Cooking Time: 16 Minutes

Ingredients:

- 2 pounds chicken wings
- 1 cup dill pickle juice
- 1 tablespoon packed dark brown sugar
- 1 tablespoon hot sauce
- ¼ teaspoon garlic salt
- ¼ teaspoon ground black pepper
- ½ cup bourbon whiskey
- 1 cup dill pickle slices

Directions:

1. In a medium bowl, combine chicken wings and pickle juice. Refrigerate 1 hour.
2. In a large bowl, combine brown sugar, hot sauce, garlic salt, and pepper. Set aside.
3. If you buy chicken wings that are connected, cut them at the joint to separate. Set aside.
4. Add chicken wings, pickle juice brine, and bourbon whiskey to the Instant Pot. Lock lid.
5. Press the Manual or Pressure Cook button and adjust time to 10 minutes. When timer beeps, let pressure release naturally for 5 minutes. Quick-release any additional pressure until float valve drops. Unlock lid.
6. Add chicken wings to spice mixture and toss. Line a baking sheet with parchment paper. Transfer wings to prepared baking sheet. Broil 3 minutes. Flip wings and broil for an additional 3 minutes.
7. Transfer wings to a plate and garnish with pickle slices. Serve warm.

Chicken Chardonnay

Servings:6

Cooking Time: 20 Minutes

Ingredients:

- 3 pounds chicken breasts, cut into 1" cubes
- 1 teaspoon fine sea salt
- 1 teaspoon ground black pepper
- 3 tablespoons olive oil
- 1 clove garlic, crushed
- 1 cup chardonnay
- 1 can diced tomatoes, including juice
- 1 cup sliced mushrooms
- 1 teaspoon dried thyme
- 1 teaspoon dried oregano

Directions:

1. On a plate, rub chicken pieces with salt and pepper.
2. Press the Sauté button on Instant Pot. Heat the oil and add garlic. Sauté for 1 minute or less, just enough to release the garlic's aroma without burning it. Pour wine and tomatoes into the Instant Pot. Press the Adjust button to change the temperature to Less and simmer unlidded for 5 minutes.
3. Arrange chicken in a single layer on top of tomato mixture in the Instant Pot. Add the mushrooms in an even layer. Sprinkle Instant Pot mixture with thyme and oregano. Lock lid.
4. Press the Manual button and adjust time to 10 minutes. When timer beeps, let pressure release naturally for 10 minutes. Quick-release any additional pressure until float valve drops and then unlock lid. Check the chicken using a meat thermometer to ensure the internal temperature is at least 165°F.
5. Using a slotted spoon, transfer chicken to a serving platter. Press the Sauté button, press the Adjust button to change the temperature to Less, and simmer sauce in Instant Pot for 5 minutes to thicken. Pour some of the sauce over chicken. Serve warm.

Buttered Chicken With Artichokes

Servings: 4

Cooking Time: 35 Minutes

Ingredients:

- 1 lb chicken breasts, chopped
- 2 artichokes, trimmed, halved
- 3 tbsp butter, melted
- 1 lemon, juiced
- Salt and pepper to taste
- 1 tbsp rosemary, chopped

Directions:

1. Heat 1 tbsp butter on Sauté in your Instant Pot and cook the chicken for a minute per side until slightly golden. Pour in 1 cup of water, seal the lid, and cook on High Pressure for 13 minutes. Do a quick release. Set aside.
2. Insert a trivet in the pot. Rub the artichoke halves with half of the lemon juice and arrange on the trivet. Seal the lid and cook on Steam for 3 minutes. Do a quick release. Combine artichoke and chicken in a large bowl. Stir in salt, pepper, and lemon juice. Drizzle the remaining butter over and sprinkle with rosemary to serve.

Chicken Wings In Yogurt-garlic Sauce

Servings: 6

Cooking Time: 35 Minutes

Ingredients:

- 12 chicken wings
- 3 tbsp olive oil
- Salt to taste
- 3 cups chicken broth
- ½ cup sour cream
- 1 cup yogurt
- 2 garlic cloves, minced

Directions:

1. Heat oil on Sauté in your Instant Pot. Brown the wings for 6 minutes, turning once. Pour in broth, salt, and seal the lid. Cook on Poultry for 15 minutes on High. Do a natural release. Unlock the lid. In a bowl, mix sour cream, yogurt, salt, and garlic. Drizzle with yogurt sauce. Serve.

Lemon & Thyme Chicken

Servings: 6

Cooking Time: 40 Minutes

Ingredients:

- 3 lb red potatoes, peeled and quartered
- 2 lb chicken thighs
- 2 tbsp olive oil
- 1 onion, chopped
- 2 garlic cloves, minced
- 2 tbsp thyme, chopped
- ¾ cup chicken broth
- 1 lemon, juiced and zested
- Salt and pepper to taste

Directions:

1. Warm the olive oil in your Instant Pot on Sauté. Place in the chicken thighs and brown for 2-3 minutes, stirring occasionally. Add in onion and garlic and cook for 3 minutes. Stir in chicken broth, lemon zest, lemon juice, potatoes, half of the thyme, salt, and pepper. Seal the lid and cook for 15 minutes on Poultry. Once ready, allow a natural release for 10 minutes and unlock the lid. Top with thyme and serve.

Spicy Honey Chicken

Servings: 4

Cooking Time: 20 Minutes

Ingredients:

- 4 chicken drumsticks
- 5 tbsp soy sauce
- 2 tbsp honey
- 1 cup chicken broth
- 1 garlic clove, minced
- 2 tbsp hot chili sauce
- 2 tbsp cornstarch
- 1 lime, cut into wedges

Directions:

1. Place soy sauce, honey, garlic, and chili sauce in your Instant Pot and stir. Add in chicken drumsticks and toss to coat. Pour in chicken broth and seal the lid. Select Manual and cook for 12 minutes on High pressure.

Mix 2 tbsp of water and cornstarch in a bowl.

2. When over, perform a quick pressure release and unlock the lid. Add in the slurry and simmer on Sauté until the sauce thickens. Serve right away with lime wedges.

Creamy Pesto Chicken

Servings:6

Cooking Time: 10 Minutes

Ingredients:

- ½ cup pesto
- ¾ cup heavy cream
- 1 tablespoon all-purpose flour
- 2 tablespoons grated Parmesan cheese
- 2 cloves garlic, peeled and minced
- ¼ teaspoon salt
- ½ teaspoon ground black pepper
- 3 pounds boneless and skinless chicken thighs
- 1 cup water

Directions:

1. In a medium bowl, whisk together pesto, cream, flour, cheese, garlic, salt, and pepper.
2. Add chicken to a 7-cup glass baking dish. Pour pesto mixture over chicken.
3. Add water to the Instant Pot and insert steam rack. Place glass baking dish on steam rack. Lock lid.
4. Press the Manual or Pressure Cook button and adjust time to 10 minutes. When timer beeps, let pressure release naturally for 10 minutes. Quick-release any additional pressure until float valve drops. Unlock lid. Check chicken using a meat thermometer to ensure internal temperature is at least 165°F.
5. Carefully remove dish from pot. Serve warm.

Moroccan-style Chicken

Servings: 4

Cooking Time: 30 Minutes

Ingredients:

- 1 lb chicken thighs, skinless
- 2 tbsp vegetable oil
- Salt and pepper to taste
- 3 garlic cloves, minced
- 1 large onion, chopped
- ¼ tsp cumin
- ½ cup chicken broth
- 12 dried apricots, sliced
- 1 lb canned tomatoes, diced
- 1 tbsp fresh ginger, grated
- ½ tsp cinnamon, ground
- 2 tbsp cilantro, chopped
- 2 tbsp flaked almonds

Directions:

1. Warm the vegetable oil in your Instant Pot on Sauté. Sprinkle chicken thighs with salt and pepper and place in the pot along with garlic and onion. Cook for 5 minutes. Stir in chicken broth, apricots, tomatoes, fresh ginger, cumin, and cinnamon. Seal the lid, select Manual, and cook for 12 minutes on High pressure. Once ready, perform a quick pressure release and unlock the lid. Serve topped with cilantro and almonds.

Tarragon Whole Chicken

Servings: 6

Cooking Time: 45 Minutes

Ingredients:

- 1 whole chicken
- 1 tsp tarragon, chopped
- 3 tbsp butter, softened
- 1 tbsp onion powder
- 1 tbsp garlic powder
- 1 tbsp paprika
- Salt and pepper to taste
- 1 cup chicken broth
- 1 tbsp white wine
- 2 tsp soy sauce

- 1 minced green onion

Directions:

1. Combine butter, tarragon, onion powder, garlic powder, paprika, salt, and pepper in a bowl. Pour the chicken broth, white wine, and soy sauce in your Instant Pot and fit in a trivet. Brush chicken with the butter mixture on all sides and place it on the trivet. Seal the lid, select Manual, and cook for 25 minutes on High pressure. When done, allow a natural release for 10 minutes and unlock the lid. Serve topped with minced green onion.

Za'atar Chicken With Baby Potatoes

Servings: 4

Cooking Time: 30 Minutes

Ingredients:

- 1 lb chicken thighs
- ½ lb baby potatoes, halved
- 2 tbsp olive oil
- 1 tbsp za'atar seasoning
- 1 garlic clove, minced
- 1 large onion, sliced
- Salt and pepper to taste

Directions:

1. Warm the olive oil in your Instant Pot on Sauté. Place in onion and garlic and cook for 2 minutes. Add in chicken thighs and cook for 4-6 minutes on both sides. Scatter with za´atar seasoning, salt, pepper, potatoes, and pour in 1 cup of water. Seal the lid, select Manual, and cook for 15 minutes on High pressure.
2. Once ready, perform a quick pressure release and unlock the lid. Remove the chicken and shred it. Put chicken back to the pot and toss to coat. Serve right away.

Fish & Seafood

Fish & Seafood

Ginger & Garlic Crab

Servings: 4

Cooking Time: 15 Minutes

Ingredients:

- 1 lb crabs, halved
- 2 tbsp butter
- 1 shallot, chopped
- 1 garlic cloves, minced
- 1 cup coconut milk
- 1-inch ginger, sliced
- 1 lemongrass stalk
- Salt and pepper to taste
- 1 lemon, sliced

Directions:

1. Melt the butter in your Instant Pot on Sauté. Place in shallot, garlic, and ginger and cook for 3 minutes. Pour in coconut milk, crabs, lemongrass, salt, and pepper and seal the lid. Select Manual and cook for 6 minutes on High pressure. Once ready, perform a quick pressure release and unlock the lid. Serve with lemon slices.

Pistachio-parm–crusted Cod

Servings: 2

Cooking Time: 7 Minutes

Ingredients:

- 2 tablespoons unsalted butter, melted
- 1 tablespoon panko bread crumbs
- 2 tablespoons chopped unsalted pistachios
- 2 tablespoons grated Parmesan cheese
- ¼ teaspoon salt
- 2 cod fillets
- 1 cup water

Directions:

1. In a small bowl, combine butter, bread crumbs, pistachios, cheese, and salt to form a thick paste.
2. Pat cod fillets dry with a paper towel. Rub paste on top of each fillet and place in steamer basket.
3. Add water to the Instant Pot and insert steam rack. Place steamer basket on steam rack. Lock lid.
4. Press the Manual or Pressure Cook button and adjust time to 5 minutes. When timer beeps, quick-release the pressure until float valve drops. Unlock lid.
5. Line a baking sheet with parchment paper. Transfer fillets to prepared baking sheet. Broil approximately 1–2 minutes until tops are browned.
6. Remove from heat and serve hot.

Lime Trout With Spinach & Tomatoes

Servings: 3

Cooking Time: 50 Minutes

Ingredients:

- 1 lb trout fillets
- 6 oz spinach, torn
- 2 tomatoes, peeled, diced
- 3 cups fish stock
- ¼ cup olive oil
- ¼ cup lime juice
- Sea salt to taste
- 2 garlic cloves, crushed

Directions:

1. Sprinkle the fillets with sea salt. In a bowl, mix olive oil and lime juice. Stir well and submerge fillets in this mixture. Refrigerate for 30 minutes; then drain the fillets. Reserve the marinade, grease the pot with 3 tbsp of the marinade, and add the fillets and stock. Seal the lid and cook on Steam for 8 minutes on High Pressure. Do a quick release. Remove the fish and set aside.
2. Add the remaining marinade to the pot. Hit Sauté and add the tomatoes and spinach. Cook until soft. Give it a good stir and remove it to a plate. Add fish, drizzle with tomato sauce and serve warm.

Rich Shrimp Risotto

Servings: 4

Cooking Time: 30 Minutes

Ingredients:

- ¾ cup Pecorino Romano cheese, grated
- 1 lb shrimp, deveined
- 4 tbsp butter
- 2 garlic cloves, minced
- 1 yellow onion, chopped
- 1 ½ cups Arborio rice
- 2 tbsp dry white wine
- 4 cups fish broth
- ½ tsp Italian seasoning
- 2 tbsp heavy cream
- Salt and pepper to taste

Directions:

1. Melt half of the butter in your Instant Pot. Add in garlic and onion and cook for 4 minutes. Stir in rice and cook for another minute. Mix in white wine and cook for 3 minutes until the wine evaporates. Pour in 3 cups of fish broth and Italian seasoning and seal the lid. Select Manual and cook for 10 minutes on High pressure.
2. When ready, perform a quick pressure release and unlock the lid. Add in shrimp and the remaining broth and cook for 4-5 minutes on Sauté. Stir in Pecorino Romano cheese, heavy cream, and the remaining butter.

Trout In Herb Sauce

Servings:4

Cooking Time: 5 Minutes

Ingredients:

- Trout
- 4 (½-pound) fresh river trout
- 1 teaspoon sea salt
- 4 cups torn lettuce leaves, divided
- 1 teaspoon white wine vinegar
- ½ cup water
- Herb Sauce
- ½ cup minced fresh flat-leaf parsley
- 2 teaspoons Italian seasoning
- 1 small shallot, peeled and minced
- 2 tablespoons mayonnaise
- ½ teaspoon fresh lemon juice
- ¼ teaspoon sugar
- Pinch of salt
- 2 tablespoons sliced almonds, toasted

Directions:

1. For Trout: Rinse the trout inside and out; pat dry. Sprinkle with salt inside and out. Put 3 cups lettuce leaves in the bottom of the Instant Pot. Arrange the trout over the top of the lettuce and top fish with the remaining lettuce.
2. Pour vinegar and water into pot. Lock lid.
3. Press the Manual button and adjust time to 3 minutes. When the timer beeps, let pressure release naturally for 3 minutes. Quick-release any additional pressure until float valve drops and then unlock lid.
4. Transfer fish to a serving plate. Peel and discard the skin from the fish. Remove and discard the heads if desired.
5. For Herb Sauce: In a small bowl, mix together the parsley, Italian seasoning, shallot, mayonnaise, lemon juice, sugar, and salt. Evenly divide among the fish, spreading it over them. Sprinkle toasted almonds over the top of the sauce. Serve.

Octopus & Shrimp With Collard Greens

Servings: 4

Cooking Time: 30 Minutes

Ingredients:

- 6 oz octopus, cut into bite-sized pieces
- 1 lb collard greens, chopped
- 1 lb shrimp, whole
- 1 tomato, chopped
- 3 cups fish stock
- 4 tbsp olive oil
- 3 garlic cloves
- 2 tbsp parsley, chopped
- 1 tsp sea salt

Directions:

1. Place shrimp and octopus in the pot. Add tomato and fish stock. Seal the lid and cook on High Pressure for 15 minutes. Do a quick release. Remove shrimp and octopus. Drain the liquid. Heat olive oil on Sauté and add garlic and parsley and cook for 1 minute. Add in collard greens, season with salt, and simmer for 5 minutes. Serve with shrimp and octopus.

Steamed Shrimp And Asparagus

Servings:2

Cooking Time: 1 Minute

Ingredients:

- 1 cup water
- 1 bunch asparagus
- 1 teaspoon sea salt, divided
- 1 pound shrimp, peeled and deveined
- ½ lemon
- 2 tablespoons butter, cut into 2 pats

Directions:

1. Pour water into Instant Pot. Insert trivet. Place steamer basket onto trivet.
2. Prepare asparagus by finding the natural snap point on the stalks and discarding the woody ends.
3. Spread the asparagus on the bottom of the steamer basket. Sprinkle with ½ teaspoon salt. Add the shrimp. Squeeze lemon into the Instant Pot, then sprinkle shrimp with remaining ½ teaspoon salt. Place pats of butter on shrimp. Lock lid.
4. Press the Manual button and adjust time to 1 minute. When the timer beeps, quick-release the pressure until the float valve drops and then unlock lid.
5. Transfer shrimp and asparagus to a platter and serve.

Salmon Fillets With Orange Sauce

Servings: 4

Cooking Time: 30 Minutes

Ingredients:

- 1 lb salmon fillets
- 1 cup orange juice
- 2 tbsp cornstarch
- Salt and pepper to taste
- 1 garlic clove, minced
- 1 tsp orange zest

Directions:

1. Combine orange juice, cornstarch, salt, pepper, garlic, orange zest, and salmon in a large bowl. Cover and let to marinate for 10-15 minutes. Then, add to the pot and seal the lid. Cook on High pressure for 10 minutes. Do a quick pressure release. Serve.

Steamed Crab Legs

Servings:2

Cooking Time: 3 Minutes

Ingredients:

- 1 cup water
- 4 cloves garlic, quartered
- 1 small onion, peeled and diced large
- 1 tablespoon Old Bay Seasoning
- 2 sprigs fresh thyme
- 2 pounds crab legs

Directions:

1. Add water, garlic, onion, Old Bay Seasoning, and thyme to the Instant Pot; stir to combine.
2. Insert trivet. Add crab legs. Lock lid.
3. Press the Steam button and adjust time to 3 minutes. When the timer beeps, quick-release the pressure until float valve drops and then unlock lid.
4. Transfer crab legs to a serving platter.

Italian Steamed Sea Bream With Lemon

Servings: 4

Cooking Time: 50 Minutes

Ingredients:

- 2 pieces sea bream, cleaned
- ¼ cup olive oil
- ¼ cup lemon juice
- 1 tbsp fresh thyme sprigs
- 1 tbsp Italian seasoning
- ½ tsp sea salt
- 1 tsp garlic powder
- 4 cups fish stock

Directions:

1. In a bowl, mix oil, lemon juice, thyme, Italian seasoning, sea salt, and garlic powder. Brush onto fish and wrap tightly with a plastic foil. Refrigerate for 30 minutes. Pour fish stock into the pot. Set the steamer rack and place the fish on top. Seal the lid. Cook on Steam for 8 minutes on High. Do a quick release. Unwrap the fish. Serve immediately with steam vegetables.

Creamed Crab Sauce

Servings:4

Cooking Time: 5 Minutes

Ingredients:

- 2 tablespoons unsalted butter
- ¼ cup finely diced red onion
- 1 pound lump crabmeat
- ¼ cup chicken broth
- 6 ounces cream cheese, softened
- 2 teaspoons cooking sherry
- 1 tablespoon all-purpose flour
- ½ teaspoon salt
- ½ teaspoon ground black pepper

Directions:

1. Press the Sauté button on the Instant Pot. Add butter and heat until melted. Add onion; stir-fry 3–5 minutes until onions begin to soften.
2. Stir crabmeat and broth into pot. Press the Cancel button. Lock lid.
3. Press the Steam button on the Instant Pot and adjust time to 0 minutes. When timer beeps, quick-release pressure until float valve drops. Unlock lid.
4. Stir in cream cheese, sherry, flour, salt, and pepper. Transfer to a serving bowl. Let sit 10 minutes to thicken. Serve warm.

Lobster Risotto

Servings:4

Cooking Time: 20 Minutes

Ingredients:

- 4 tablespoons butter
- 1 small onion, peeled and finely diced
- 2 cloves garlic, minced
- 1½ cups Arborio rice
- 1 cup chardonnay
- 3 cups vegetable broth
- ½ teaspoon lemon zest
- 3 tablespoons grated Parmesan cheese
- ½ teaspoon salt
- ¼ teaspoon ground black pepper
- Meat from 3 small lobster tails, diced
- ¼ cup chopped fresh parsley

Directions:

1. Press the Sauté button on the Instant Pot and add the butter. Heat until melted. Add onion and stir-fry for 3–5 minutes until translucent. Add garlic and rice and cook for an additional minute. Add white wine and slowly stir unlidded for 5 minutes until liquid is absorbed by the rice.
2. Add broth, lemon zest, Parmesan, salt, and pepper. Lock lid.
3. Press the Rice button. Let pressure release naturally for 10 minutes. Quick-release any additional pressure until float valve drops and then unlock lid.
4. Stir in lobster, garnish with fresh parsley, and serve warm.

Beer-steamed Mussels

Servings: 4

Cooking Time: 15 Minutes

Ingredients:

- 3 lb mussels, debearded
- 4 tbsp butter
- 1 shallot, chopped
- 2 garlic cloves, minced
- 2 tbsp parsley, chopped
- 1 cup beer
- 1 cup chicken stock

Directions:

1. Melt butter in your Instant Pot on Sauté. Add in shallot and garlic and cook for 2 minutes. Stir in beer and cook for 1 minute. Mix in stock and mussels and seal the lid.
2. Select Manual and cook for 3 minutes on High pressure. Once ready, perform a quick pressure release. Discard unopened mussels. Serve sprinkled with parsley.

Crab Pilaf With Broccoli & Asparagus

Servings: 4

Cooking Time: 30 Minutes

Ingredients:

- ½ lb asparagus, trimmed and cut into 1-inch pieces
- ½ lb broccoli florets
- Salt to taste
- 2 tbsp olive oil
- 1 small onion, chopped
- 1 cup rice
- 1/3 cup white wine
- 2 cups vegetable stock
- 8 oz lump crabmeat

Directions:

1. Heat oil on Sauté and cook the onion for 3 minutes until soft. Stir in rice and cook for 1 minute. Pour in the wine. Cook for 2 to 3 minutes, stirring until the liquid has almost evaporated. Add vegetable stock and salt; stir.
2. Place a trivet on top. Arrange the broccoli and asparagus on the trivet. Seal the lid and cook on High Pressure for 8 minutes. Do a quick release. Remove the vegetables to a bowl. Fluff the rice with a fork and add in the crabmeat, heat for a minute. Taste and adjust the seasoning. Serve immediately topped with broccoli and asparagus.

Crab Risotto

Servings:4

Cooking Time: 15 Minutes

Ingredients:

- 4 tablespoons unsalted butter
- 1 small yellow onion, peeled and finely diced
- 1 ½ cups Arborio rice
- 4 cups vegetable broth
- 3 tablespoons grated Parmesan cheese, divided
- ½ teaspoon garlic salt
- ¼ teaspoon ground black pepper
- 1 cup lump crabmeat, picked over for shells

Directions:

1. Press the Sauté button on the Instant Pot. Add butter and heat until melted. Add onion and stir-fry 3–5 minutes until translucent.
2. Add rice, broth, 2 tablespoons cheese, garlic salt, and pepper. Press the Cancel button. Lock lid.
3. Press the Manual or Pressure Cook button and adjust time to 10 minutes. When timer beeps, let pressure release naturally for 10 minutes. Quick-release any additional pressure until float valve drops. Unlock lid.
4. Stir in crab and remaining cheese. Serve warm.

Tangy Shrimp Curry

Servings: 4

Cooking Time: 15 Minutes

Ingredients:

- 1 lb shrimp, deveined
- 2 tbsp sesame oil
- 1 onion, chopped
- ½ tsp fresh ginger, grated
- 1 garlic clove, minced
- 1 tsp cayenne pepper
- 1 tbsp lime juice
- 1 cup coconut milk
- 1 tbsp curry powder
- Salt and pepper to taste

Directions:

1. Heat the sesame oil in your Instant Pot on Sauté and cook the onion, garlic, and ginger for 3-4 minutes. Stir in curry powder, cayenne pepper, salt, and pepper and cook for 3 minutes. Pour in coconut milk, shrimp, and 1 cup of water and seal the lid. Select Manual and cook for 4 minutes on Low pressure. Once done, perform a quick pressure release. Drizzle with lime juice and serve.

Rosemary Cod With Cherry Tomatoes

Servings: 4

Cooking Time: 25 Minutes

Ingredients:

- 1 ½ lb cod fillets
- 3 tbsp butter
- 1 onion, sliced
- 2 garlic cloves, minced
- ½ lb cherry tomatoes, halved
- 1 lemon juice
- Salt and pepper to taste
- 2 tbsp rosemary, chopped
- 1 cup vegetable broth

Directions:

1. Melt the butter in your Instant Pot on Sauté. Add in the onion, garlic, and rosemary and sauté for 3 minutes, stirring often. Add in the cod fillets and cook for 3-4 minutes on both sides. Sprinkle with salt and pepper, and cook for 3-4 minutes. Pour in vegetable broth and top with cherry tomatoes. Seal the lid, select Manual. Cook for 3 minutes on High pressure. When ready, perform a quick pressure release and unlock the lid. Top the cod with lemon juice and serve with sauce.

Pork, Beef & Lamb

Pork, Beef & Lamb

Awesome Herby Pork Butt With Yams

Servings: 4

Cooking Time: 35 Minutes

Ingredients:

- 1 lb pork butt, cut into 4 equal pieces
- 1 lb yams, diced
- 2 tsp butter
- ¼ tsp thyme
- ¼ tsp oregano
- 1 ½ tsp sage
- 1 ½ cups beef broth
- Salt and pepper to taste

Directions:

1. Season the pork with thyme, sage, oregano, salt, and pepper. Melt butter on Sauté. Add pork and cook until brown, about 5 minutes. Add the yams and pour the broth. Seal the lid and cook for 20 minutes on Meat/Stew. Do a quick release. Serve hot.

Tarragon Apple Pork Chops

Servings: 4

Cooking Time: 25 Minutes

Ingredients:

- 2 tbsp olive oil
- 1 tsp nutmeg
- 1 tsp Dijon mustard
- 4 tbsp brown sugar
- 2 Granny Smith apples, sliced
- 4 pork chops
- Salt and pepper to taste
- 2 tbsp tarragon, chopped

Directions:

1. Combine nutmeg, mustard, and brown sugar in a bowl. Add in apples and toss to coat. Warm oil in your Instant Pot on Sauté. Place the apples in the pot and cook for 2 minutes. Sprinkle pork chops with salt and pepper and put it over the apples. Seal the lid, select Manual, and cook for 15 minutes on High. Once done, perform a quick pressure release. Top with tarragon and serve.

Pork Belly With Tamari Sauce

Servings: 6

Cooking Time: 35 Minutes

Ingredients:

- 4 garlic cloves, sliced
- ½ tsp ground cloves
- 1 tsp grated fresh ginger
- 1 ½ lb pork belly, sliced
- 2 ¼ cups water
- ¼ cup white wine
- ½ cup onions, chopped
- ¼ cup tamari sauce
- 1 tsp sugar maple syrup
- 4 cups white rice, cooked
- Salt and pepper to taste

Directions:

1. Brown pork belly for about 6 minutes per side on Sauté. Add garlic, cloves, ginger, water, wine, onions, tamari sauce, maple syrup, rice, salt, and pepper. Seal the lid and cook for 25 minutes on Pressure Cook. When ready, do a quick pressure release. Serve immediately.

Savory Herb Meatloaf

Servings: 4

Cooking Time: 45 Minutes

Ingredients:

- 1 lb ground beef
- 1 egg, beaten
- 1 tsp garlic powder
- 1 tsp onion powder
- 1 shredded potato
- ½ tsp rosemary
- ½ tsp thyme
- 1 ½ tsp parsley
- Salt and pepper to taste
- Dill pickles, to serve

Directions:

1. Add the ground beef, egg, onion powder, garlic powder, shredded potato, rosemary, thyme, parsley, salt, and pepper to a bowl and combine them until everything is well mixed. Press the meatloaf mixture to a greased cooking pan. Pour 1 cup of water into your Instant Pot and fit in a trivet. Place the pan on the trivet and seal the lid. Select Manual and cook for 25 minutes on High.
2. When ready, allow a natural release for 10 minutes, then perform a quick pressure release, and unlock the lid. Remove the meatloaf to a plate and let cool before slicing. Serve with dill pickles.

Beef & Vegetable Stew

Servings: 6

Cooking Time: 55 Minutes

Ingredients:

- 2 lb beef stew meat, cubed
- Salt and pepper to taste
- ½ tsp onion powder
- 1/3 cup flour
- 1 tsp Italian seasoning
- 2 tbsp olive oil
- 1 onion, chopped
- 3 garlic cloves, minced
- 1 tbsp red wine
- 1 tbsp tomato paste
- 4 potatoes, peeled, chopped
- 1 cup green beans, trimmed
- 1 tsp paprika
- 1 cup tomatoes, chopped
- 1 celery rib, chopped
- 2 carrots, sliced
- 3 cups beef broth
- 1 bay leaf
- 2 tbsp parsley, chopped

Directions:

1. Combine salt, pepper, onion powder, flour, and Italian seasoning in a bowl. Add in beef meat and toss to coat. Warm the olive oil in your Instant Pot on Sauté. Place the meat in the pot and cook for 5-6 minutes, stirring occasionally; set aside. Place the onion, garlic, celery, carrot, and paprika in the pot and cook for 3-4 minutes.
2. Pour in wine and scrape any brown bits from the bottom. Put the meat back to the pot and tomato paste, tomatoes, potatoes, green beans, broth, bay leaf, salt, and pepper and stir. Seal the lid, select Manual, and cook for 25 minutes on High. When ready, allow a natural release for 10 minutes. Serve topped with parsley.

Pork With Onions & Cream Sauce

Servings: 6

Cooking Time: 52 Minutes

Ingredients:

- 1 ½ lb pork shoulder, cut into pieces
- 2 onions, chopped
- 1 ½ cups sour cream
- 1 cup tomato puree
- ½ tbsp cilantro
- ¼ tsp cumin
- ¼ tsp cayenne pepper
- 1 garlic clove, minced
- Salt and pepper to taste

Directions:

1. Coat with cooking spray the inner pot and add the pork. Cook for 3-4 minutes on Sauté until lightly browned. Add onions and garlic and cook for 3 minutes until fragrant. Press Cancel. Stir in sour cream, tomato puree, cilantro, cumin, cayenne pepper, salt, and pepper and seal the lid. Select Soup/Broth and cook for 30 minutes on High. Let sit for 5 minutes before quickly release the pressure.

Fennel & Rosemary Pork Belly

Servings: 2

Cooking Time: 60 Minutes

Ingredients:

- 1 lb pork belly
- 2 tbsp olive oil
- ¼ tsp ground cinnamon
- ¼ tsp chili flakes
- 1 tsp fennel seeds
- 1 rosemary sprig
- 1 clove garlic, minced
- 1 cup red wine
- Salt and pepper to taste
- 2 tbsp chopped chives

Directions:

1. Warm the olive oil in your Instant Pot on Sauté. Place the pork belly and cook 4 minutes on both sides. Add in salt, pepper, garlic, fennel seeds, cinnamon, rosemary sprig, chili flakes, red wine, and 1 cup of water. Seal the lid, select Manual, and cook for 35 minutes on High.
2. Once over, allow a natural release for 10 minutes, then perform a quick pressure release, and unlock the lid. Cut the pork and scatter with chives. Serve warm.

Roast Lamb Leg With Potatoes

Servings: 6

Cooking Time: 35 Minutes

Ingredients:

- 2 lb lamb leg
- 2 garlic cloves
- 1 tbsp thyme, chopped
- 1 lb potatoes
- 1 lemon, chopped
- 3 tbsp oil
- ¼ cup red wine vinegar
- 1 tsp brown sugar
- 1 tsp salt

Directions:

1. Place the potatoes in the pot, and pour enough water to cover. Season with salt, add garlic, and seal the lid. Set to Meat/Stew. Cook for 20 minutes on High Pressure. Do a quick release and remove potatoes; reserve the liquid.
2. Rub the meat with oil and thyme. Place in the pot. Pour in red wine vinegar, sugar, and add lemon. Add 1 cup of the reserved liquid and seal the lid. Cook on High Pressure for 7 minutes. Do a quick release.

Short Ribs With Wine Mushroom Sauce

Servings: 4

Cooking Time: 75 Minutes

Ingredients:

- 2 lb boneless pork short ribs, cut into 3-inch pieces
- Salt and pepper to taste
- ½ onion, chopped
- ½ cup red wine
- 3 tbsp olive oil
- ½ tbsp tomato paste
- 2 carrots, sliced
- 2 cups mushrooms, sliced
- 1 tbsp cornstarch
- Minced parsley to garnish

Directions:

1. Rub the ribs on all sides with salt and pepper. Heat the oil on Sauté in your Instant Pot and brown short ribs on all sides, about 6-7 minutes. Remove to a plate. Add onion to the pot and cook for 3-5 minutes. Pour in wine and tomato paste to deglaze by scraping any browned bits from the bottom of the cooker. Cook for 2 minutes until the wine has reduced slightly. Return ribs to the pot and cover with carrots. Pour 1 cup of water over.
2. Seal the lid, and select Manual on High Pressure for 35 minutes. When ready, let the pressure release naturally for 10 minutes. Carefully unlock the lid. Transfer ribs and carrots to a plate. To the pot, add mushrooms. Press Sauté and cook them for 2-4 minutes. In a bowl, add 2 tbsp of water and cornstarch and mix until smooth. Pour this slurry into the pot, stirring constantly until it thickens slightly, 2 minutes. Season the gravy with salt and pepper. Pour over the ribs and garnish with parsley.

Pizza Dogs

Servings:4

Cooking Time: 3 Minutes

Ingredients:

- 2 cups water
- 8 beef hot dogs
- 8 hot dog buns
- 1 cup jarred pizza sauce
- 1 cup shredded mozzarella
- 32 mini pepperoni pieces

Directions:

1. Add water to the Instant Pot. Add hot dogs. Lock lid.
2. Press the Manual or Pressure Cook button and adjust time to 0 minutes. When timer beeps, quick-release pressure until float valve drops. Unlock lid.
3. Preheat oven to broiler to 500°F. Assemble Pizza Dogs by adding a hot dog to each bun. Add sauce and cheese evenly to each one. Add 4 pepperoni pieces to each. Place assembled dogs on a parchment paper–lined baking sheet. Broil 2–3 minutes until cheese is melted. Serve warm.

Beef Bones With Beans & Chili Pepper

Servings: 4

Cooking Time: 30 Minutes

Ingredients:

- 14.5 oz canned beans
- 12 oz beef bones
- 1 onion, chopped
- 3 garlic cloves
- 1 carrot, chopped
- 1 tbsp parsley, chopped
- 1 bay leaf
- Salt and pepper to taste
- 1 chili pepper, minced
- 3 tbsp vegetable oil

Directions:

1. Place beans, beef bones, onion, garlic, carrot, parsley, bay leaf, salt, pepper, chili pepper, and oil in the Instant Pot. Pour water enough to cover. Seal the lid. Cook on High Pressure for 15 minutes. Release the steam naturally for 10 minutes. Let it chill for a while before serving.

Friday Night Bbq Pork Butt

Servings: 6

Cooking Time: 55 Minutes

Ingredients:

- 2 lb pork butt
- Salt and pepper to taste
- 1 cup barbecue sauce
- ¼ tsp cumin powder
- ½ tsp onion powder
- 1 ½ cups beef broth

Directions:

1. In a bowl, combine the barbecue sauce, cumin, onion powder, salt, and pepper. Brush the pork with the mixture. On Sauté, coat with cooking oil. Add the pork and sear on all sides for 6 minutes. Pour the beef broth around the meat. Seal the lid and cook for 40 minutes on Meat/Stew on High. Do the pressure quickly. Serve.

Barbecue Flank Steak Taco Filling

Servings:4

Cooking Time: 45 Minutes

Ingredients:

- ¼ cup ketchup
- ¼ cup apricot preserves
- ⅛ cup honey
- ⅛ cup apple cider vinegar
- ¼ cup soy sauce
- ⅛ teaspoon cayenne pepper
- 1 teaspoon ground mustard
- ¼ teaspoon ground black pepper
- 1 flank steak
- 2 tablespoons avocado oil, divided
- 1 large sweet onion, peeled and sliced
- 1½ cups beef broth

Directions:

1. In a small bowl, combine ketchup, preserves, honey, vinegar, soy sauce, cayenne pepper, mustard, and pepper. Spread mixture on all sides of the flank steak.
2. Press the Sauté button on Instant Pot. Heat 1 tablespoon oil. Sear meat on each side for approximately 5 minutes. Remove the meat and set aside. Add remaining 1 tablespoon oil and onions. Sauté onions for 3–5 minutes until translucent.
3. Add beef broth. Set meat and all of the sauce on the layer of onions. Lock lid.
4. Press the Meat button and adjust time to 35 minutes. When timer beeps, let pressure release naturally until float valve drops and then unlock lid.
5. Transfer the meat to a serving platter. Thinly slice against the grain and serve immediately.

Beef & Root Vegetable Pot

Servings: 4

Cooking Time: 65 Minutes

Ingredients:

- 1 lb beef stew meat, cubed
- 2 tbsp olive oil
- Salt and pepper to taste
- 1 leek, chopped
- 2 garlic cloves, minced
- 1 tsp dried thyme
- 2 tbsp flour
- 1 cup dry red wine
- 2 cups chopped tomatoes
- 1 turnip, chopped
- 1 lb sweet potatoes, sliced
- 2 carrots, chopped
- 2 cups beef broth
- ¼ cup parsley, chopped

Directions:

1. Warm the olive oil in your Instant Pot on Sauté. Sprinkle beef meat with salt and pepper and place it in the pot. Sauté for 6-7 minutes on all sides until browned; set aside. Add leek and garlic to the pot and cook for 3 minutes. Stir in thyme and flour and cook for 1 minute. Pour in red wine and scrape any brown bits from the bottom.
2. Add in turnip, carrots, sweet potatoes, tomatoes, and beef broth. Put the meat back to the pot and seal the lid. Select Manual and cook for 30 minutes on High pressure. Once over, allow a natural release for 10 minutes and unlock the lid. Serve topped with parsley.

Dry-rubbed Baby Back Ribs

Servings:4

Cooking Time: 25 Minutes

Ingredients:

- 1 teaspoon garlic salt
- 1 teaspoon chili powder
- 1 teaspoon ground black pepper
- ½ teaspoon ground mustard
- ½ teaspoon onion powder
- 1 teaspoon instant espresso coffee
- 2 racks pork baby back ribs, cut into 2-rib sections
- 2 cups water
- 1 tablespoon olive oil

Directions:

1. In a small bowl, combine garlic salt, chili powder, pepper, ground mustard, onion powder, and espresso coffee. Massage mixture into rib sections. Refrigerate covered at least 1 hour or up to overnight.
2. Add water to the Instant Pot and insert steam rack. Place steamer basket on top. Place ribs standing upright in basket with meaty side facing outward toward pot wall. Lock lid.
3. Press the Manual or Pressure Cook button and adjust time to 25 minutes. When timer beeps, let pressure release naturally until float valve drops. Unlock lid.
4. Transfer ribs to a platter and drizzle with oil. Serve warm.

Balsamic Lamb

Servings: 4

Cooking Time: 45 Minutes

Ingredients:

- 2 lb lamb shanks
- 2 tbsp sesame oil
- 2 garlic cloves, peeled
- 1 onion, chopped
- 1 cup vegetable broth
- 1 tbsp tomato paste
- ½ tsp thyme
- ¼ tsp dried dill weed
- 1 tbsp balsamic vinegar
- 1 tbsp butter

Directions:

1. Warm sesame oil in your Instant Pot on Sauté. Place in onion and garlic and sauté for 3 minutes. Stir in broth, tomato paste, dill, and thyme. Add in the lamb and seal the lid. Select Manual and cook for 25 minutes on High.
2. When ready, allow a natural release for 5 minutes and unlock the lid. Remove the lamb to a bowl. Stir the balsamic vinegar and butter in the pot for 1-2 minutes until the butter melts. Serve the lamb with sauce.

German Pork With Sauerkraut

Servings: 4

Cooking Time: 40 Minutes

Ingredients:

- 2 lb pork belly, cut into 2-inch pieces
- 3 tbsp lard
- 2 garlic cloves, minced
- 1 onion, chopped
- 1 cup chicken broth
- 5 cups sauerkraut
- 1 tsp paprika
- 1 cup canned diced tomatoes
- 1 tsp cumin
- 2 tbsp parsley, chopped
- Salt and pepper to taste

Directions:

1. Sprinkle the pork with salt and pepper. Melt lard in your Instant Pot on Sauté. Place the pork, onion, and garlic and cook for 5-6 minutes. Stir in paprika and cumin. Put in sauerkraut, chicken broth, tomatoes, and 1/2 cup of water and seal the lid. Select Manual and cook for 30 minutes on High pressure. Once over, perform a quick pressure release and unlock the lid. Serve with parsley.

Delicious Pork In Button Mushroom Gravy

Servings: 6

Cooking Time: 60 Minutes

Ingredients:

- 1 cup button mushrooms, chopped
- Salt and garlic powder to taste
- 2 lb pork shoulder
- 2 tbsp butter, unsalted
- 1 tbsp balsamic vinegar
- ¼ cup soy sauce
- 2 bay leaves
- 1 cup beef broth
- 2 tbsp cornstarch

Directions:

1. Rub the pork with salt and garlic powder. Melt butter on Sauté. Brown the meat for 5 minutes on each side. Stir in soy sauce and bay leaves. Cook for 2 minutes. Add in beef broth and balsamic vinegar. Seal the lid and set to Meat/Stew. Cook for 30 minutes on High Pressure.

2. When done, do a quick release. Remove and discard the bay leaves. Stir in mushrooms. Cook for about 8 minutes on Sauté. Stir in cornstarch and cook for 2 minutes.

Pulled Pork With Homemade Bbq Sauce

Servings: 6

Cooking Time: 70 Minutes

Ingredients:

- 2 lb pork shoulder
- 1 tbsp onion powder
- 1 tbsp garlic powder
- Salt and pepper to taste
- 1 tbsp chili powder
- 2 cups vegetable stock
- 6 dates, soaked
- ¼ cup tomato paste
- ½ cup coconut aminos

Directions:

1. In a small bowl, combine onion powder, garlic powder, salt, black pepper, and chili powder. Rub the mixture onto the pork. Place the pork inside your pressure cooker. Pour the stock around the meat, not over it, and then seal the lid. Select Pressure Cook and set the timer to 60 minutes. Place the dates, tomato paste, and coconut aminos in a food processor; pulse until smooth. Release the pressure quickly. Grab two forks and shred the meat inside the pot. Pour the sauce over and stir to combine.

Desserts & Drinks

Desserts & Drinks

Peachy Crisp

Servings: 4

Cooking Time: 12 Minutes

Ingredients:

- 3 cups peeled, pitted, and diced peaches
- 4 tablespoons unsalted butter, melted
- ½ cup old-fashioned oats
- ⅛ cup all-purpose flour
- ¼ cup chopped almonds
- ⅓ cup granulated sugar
- ¼ teaspoon ground allspice
- ¼ teaspoon salt
- 1 cup water

Directions:

1. Place peaches in a 7-cup glass baking dish.
2. In a food processor, pulse together butter, oats, flour, almonds, sugar, allspice, and salt until butter is well distributed.
3. Preheat oven to broiler at 500°F.
4. Add water to the Instant Pot and insert steam rack. Lower glass baking dish onto steam rack. Lock lid.
5. Press the Manual or Pressure Cook button and adjust time to 8 minutes. When timer beeps, let pressure release naturally until float valve drops. Unlock lid.
6. Place dish under broiler 3–4 minutes until browned.
7. Serve warm or chilled.

Classic French Squash Tart

Servings: 6

Cooking Time: 35 Minutes

Ingredients:

- 15 oz mashed squash
- 6 fl oz milk
- ½ tsp cinnamon, ground
- ½ tsp nutmeg
- ½ tsp salt
- 3 large eggs
- ½ cup granulated sugar
- 1 pack pate brisee

Directions:

1. Place squash puree in a large bowl. Add milk, cinnamon, eggs, nutmeg, salt, and sugar. Whisk together until well incorporated. Grease a baking dish with oil. Gently place pate brisee creating the edges with hands. Pour the squash mixture over and flatten the surface with a spatula. Pour 1 cup of water into the pot and insert the trivet. Lay the baking dish on the trivet. Seal the lid, and cook for 25 minutes on High Pressure. Do a quick release. Transfer the pie to a serving platter. Refrigerate.

Catalan-style Crème Brûlée

Servings: 4

Cooking Time: 15 Minutes

Ingredients:

- 5 cups heavy cream
- 8 egg yolks
- 1 cup honey
- 4 tbsp sugar
- 1 vanilla extract
- 1 cup water

Directions:

1. In a bowl, combine heavy cream, egg yolks, vanilla, and honey. Beat well with an electric mixer. Pour the mixture into 4 ramekins. Set aside. Pour water into the pot and insert the trivet. Lower the ramekins on top. Seal the lid and cook for 10 minutes on High Pressure. Do a quick pressure release. Remove the ramekins from the pot and add a tablespoon of sugar to each ramekin. Burn evenly with a culinary torch until brown. Chill well and serve.

Blueberry-orange Quick Jam

Servings:4

Cooking Time: 7 Minutes

Ingredients:

- 1 pound fresh blueberries
- 1 cup granulated sugar
- Juice and zest from ½ medium orange
- ⅛ teaspoon salt
- ½ cup water, divided
- 2 tablespoons cornstarch

Directions:

1. Add blueberries, sugar, orange juice and zest, salt, and ¼ cup water to the Instant Pot. Lock lid.
2. Press the Manual or Pressure Cook button and adjust time to 4 minutes. When timer beeps, let pressure release naturally for 10 minutes. Quick-release any additional pressure until float valve drops. Press the Cancel button. Unlock lid.
3. Create a slurry by whisking together remaining ¼ cup water and cornstarch.
4. Add slurry to berry mixture to thicken, smooshing blueberries against sides of pot as you stir.
5. Press the Sauté button on the Instant Pot and cook an additional 3 minutes. Allow mixture to cool for at least 30 minutes until it reaches room temperature.
6. Transfer jam to an airtight container and refrigerate until ready to eat. Serve warmed or chilled.

Hot Cocoa Brownies

Servings:6

Cooking Time: 25 Minutes

Ingredients:

- 2 large eggs, beaten
- ¼ cup all-purpose flour
- 2 packets instant hot cocoa mix
- ⅓ cup granulated sugar
- 2 teaspoons baking powder
- 1 teaspoon baking soda
- ⅛ teaspoon salt
- 4 tablespoons unsalted butter, melted
- ⅓ cup mini marshmallows
- 1 cup water

Directions:

1. Grease a 6" cake pan.
2. In a large bowl, combine eggs, flour, hot cocoa mix, sugar, baking powder, baking soda, and salt. Stir in butter and then fold in mini marshmallows. Do not overmix. Pour batter into prepared cake pan.
3. Add water to the Instant Pot and insert steam rack. Place cake pan on top of steam rack. Lock lid.
4. Press the Manual or Pressure Cook button and adjust time to 25 minutes. When timer beeps, let pressure release naturally for 10 minutes. Quick-release any additional pressure until float valve drops. Unlock lid.
5. Remove cake pan from pot and transfer to a cooling rack to cool 10 minutes.
6. Flip brownies onto a serving platter. Let cool completely 30 minutes. Slice and serve.

Peanut Butter Custards

Servings:4

Cooking Time: 18 Minutes

Ingredients:

- 4 large egg yolks
- 2 tablespoons granulated sugar
- ⅛ teaspoon salt
- ¼ teaspoon vanilla extract
- 1 ½ cups heavy whipping cream
- ¾ cup peanut butter chips

- 2 cups water

Directions:

1. In a small bowl, whisk together egg yolks, sugar, salt, and vanilla. Set aside.
2. In a small saucepan over medium-low heat, heat cream to a low simmer, about 2 minutes. Whisk a spoonful of warm cream mixture into egg mixture to temper eggs. Then slowly add egg mixture back into saucepan with remaining cream.
3. Add peanut butter chips and continually stir on simmer until chips are melted, about 8–10 minutes. Remove from heat and evenly distribute mixture among four custard ramekins.
4. Add water to the Instant Pot and insert steam rack. Place steamer basket on steam rack. Place ramekins into basket. Lock lid.
5. Press the Manual or Pressure Cook button and adjust time to 6 minutes. When timer beeps, let pressure release naturally for 10 minutes. Quick-release any additional pressure until float valve drops. Unlock lid.
6. Transfer ramekins to a plate and refrigerate covered at least 2 hours or up to overnight. Serve chilled.

Simple Apple Cider With Orange Juice

Servings: 6

Cooking Time: 20 Minutes

Ingredients:

- 6 green apples, chopped
- ¼ cup orange juice
- 2 cinnamon sticks

Directions:

1. In a blender, add orange juice, apples, and 3 cups water and blend until smooth; use a fine-mesh strainer to strain and press using a spoon. Get rid of the pulp. In the pot, mix the apple puree and cinnamon sticks. Seal the lid and cook for 10 minutes on High Pressure. Release the Pressure naturally. Strain again and do away with the solids.

Cinnamon Brown Rice Pudding

Servings: 4

Cooking Time: 25 Minutes

Ingredients:

- 1 cup short-grain brown rice
- 1⅓ cups water
- 1 tablespoon vanilla extract
- 1 cinnamon stick
- 1 tablespoon butter
- 1 cup raisins
- 3 tablespoons honey
- ½ cup heavy cream

Directions:

1. Add rice, water, vanilla, cinnamon stick, and butter to Instant Pot. Lock lid.
2. Press the Manual button and adjust time to 20 minutes. When timer beeps, let pressure release naturally for 10 minutes. Quick-release any additional pressure until float valve drops and then unlock lid.
3. Remove the cinnamon stick and discard. Stir in the raisins, honey, and cream.
4. Press Sauté button on Instant Pot, press Adjust button to change the temperature to Less, and simmer unlidded for 5 minutes. Serve warm.

Yogurt Cheesecake With Cranberries

Servings: 6

Cooking Time: 45 Minutes + Chilling Time

Ingredients:

- 2 lb Greek yogurt
- 2 cups sugar
- 4 eggs
- 2 tsp lemon zest
- 1 tsp lemon extract
- 1 cheesecake crust
- For topping:
- 7 oz dried cranberries
- 2 tbsp cranberry jam
- 2 tsp lemon zest
- 1 tsp vanilla sugar
- 1 tsp cranberry extract

- ¾ cup lukewarm water

Directions:

1. In a bowl, combine yogurt, sugar, eggs, lemon zest, and lemon extract. With a mixer, beat well until well-combined. Place the crust in a greased cake pan and pour in the filling. Flatten the surface with a spatula. Leave in the fridge for 30 minutes. Combine cranberries, jam, lemon zest, vanilla sugar, cranberry extract, and water in the pot. Simmer for 15 minutes on Sauté. Remove and wipe the pot clean. Fill in 1 cup water and insert a trivet. Set the pan on top of the trivet and pour cranberry topping. Seal the lid and cook for 20 minutes on High Pressure. Do a quick release. Run a sharp knife around the edge of the cheesecake. Refrigerate. Serve and enjoy!

Simple Apple Cinnamon Dessert

Servings: 6

Cooking Time: 30 Minutes

Ingredients:

- Topping:
- ½ cup rolled oats
- ½ cup oat flour
- ½ cup granulated sugar
- ¼ cup olive oil
- Filling:
- 5 apples, cored, and halved
- 2 tbsp arrowroot powder
- ½ cup water
- 1 tsp ground cinnamon
- ¼ tsp ground nutmeg
- ½ tsp vanilla paste

Directions:

1. In a bowl, combine sugar, oat flour, rolled oats, and olive oil to form coarse crumbs. Spoon the apples into the Instant Pot. Mix water with arrowroot powder in a bowl. Stir in nutmeg, cinnamon, and vanilla. Toss in the apples to coat. Apply oat topping to the apples. Seal the lid and cook on High Pressure for 10 minutes. Release the pressure naturally for 10 minutes.

Chocolate Custard

Servings:4

Cooking Time: 20 Minutes

Ingredients:

- 4 large egg yolks
- 2 tablespoons sugar
- Pinch of salt
- ¼ teaspoon vanilla extract
- 1½ cups half-and-half
- ¾ cup semisweet chocolate chips
- 2 cups water

Directions:

1. In a small bowl, whisk together egg yolks, sugar, salt, and vanilla. Set aside.
2. In saucepan over medium-low heat, heat half-and-half to a low simmer. Whisk a spoonful into the egg mixture to temper the eggs, then slowly add the egg mixture back into the saucepan with remaining half-and-half. Add chocolate chips and continually stir on simmer until chocolate is melted, about 10 minutes. Remove from heat and evenly distribute chocolate mixture among four custard ramekins.
3. Pour water into Instant Pot. Insert trivet. Place silicone steamer basket onto trivet. Place ramekins onto steamer basket. Lock lid.
4. Press the Manual button and adjust time to 6 minutes. When timer beeps, let pressure release naturally for 10 minutes. Quick-release any additional pressure until float valve drops and then unlock lid.
5. Transfer custards to a plate and refrigerate covered for 2 hours. Serve.

Chocolate Chip Cheesecake

Servings:6

Cooking Time: 30 Minutes

Ingredients:

- Crust
- 22 chocolate wafer cookies
- 4 tablespoons unsalted butter, melted
- Cheesecake Filling
- 14 ounces cream cheese, cubed and softened
- ½ cup granulated sugar
- ⅛ teaspoon salt
- 2 large eggs, room temperature
- ½ cup mini semisweet chocolate chips
- 1 cup water

Directions:

1. Grease a 7" springform pan and set aside.
2. Add chocolate wafers to a food processor and pulse to combine. Add in butter. Pulse to blend. Transfer crumb mixture to prepared springform pan and press down along the bottom and about ⅓ of the way up sides of pan. Place a square of aluminum foil along the outside bottom of pan and crimp up around edges.
3. With a hand blender or food processor, cream together cream cheese, sugar, and salt. Pulse until smooth. Slowly add eggs. Pulse another 10 seconds. Scrape bowl and pulse until batter is smooth. Fold in chocolate chips.
4. Pour mixture over crust in springform pan.
5. Add water to the Instant Pot and insert steam rack. Set springform pan on steam rack. Lock lid.
6. Press the Manual or Pressure Cook button and adjust time to 30 minutes. When timer beeps, quick-release pressure until float valve drops. Unlock lid.
7. Lift pan out of pot. Let cool at room temperature 10 minutes. The cheesecake will be a little jiggly in the center. Refrigerate a minimum of 2 hours or up to overnight to allow it to set. Release sides of pan and serve.

Banana & Walnut Oatmeal

Servings: 2

Cooking Time: 20 Minutes

Ingredients:

- 1 banana, chopped
- 1 cup rolled oats
- 1 cup milk
- ¼ teaspoon cinnamon
- 1 tbsp chopped walnuts
- ½ tsp white sugar

Directions:

1. Pour 1 cup of water into your Instant Pot and fit in a steam rack. Place oats, sugar, milk, cinnamon, and ½ of water in a bowl. Divide between small-sized cups. Place on the steam rack. Seal the lid, select Manual, and cook for 5 minutes on High pressure. When done, allow a natural release for 10 minutes and unlock the lid. Top with banana and walnuts and serve.

Peanut Butter Chocolate Cheesecake

Servings:6

Cooking Time: 30 Minutes

Ingredients:

- Crust
- 20 vanilla wafers
- 2 tablespoons creamy peanut butter
- 3 tablespoons melted butter
- Cheesecake Filling
- 12 ounces cream cheese, cubed and room temperature
- 2 tablespoons sour cream, room temperature
- ½ cup sugar
- ¼ cup unsweetened cocoa
- 2 large eggs, room temperature
- 1 teaspoon vanilla extract
- 2 cups water
- ¼ cup mini semisweet chocolate chips
- ¼ cup chopped peanuts
- 2 tablespoons chocolate syrup
- 1 cup whipped cream

Directions:

1. For Crust: Grease a 7" springform pan and set aside.
2. Add vanilla wafers to a food processor and pulse to combine. Add in peanut butter and melted butter. Pulse to blend. Transfer crumb mixture to springform pan and press down along the bottom and about ⅓ of the way up the sides of the pan. Place a square of aluminum foil along the outside bottom of the pan and crimp up around the edges.
3. For Cheesecake Filling: With a hand blender or food processor, cream together cream cheese, sour cream, sugar, and cocoa. Pulse until smooth. Slowly add eggs and vanilla extract. Pulse for another 10 seconds. Scrape the bowl and pulse until batter is smooth. Transfer the batter into springform pan.
4. Pour water into the Instant Pot. Insert the trivet. Set the springform pan on the trivet. Lock lid.
5. Press the Manual button and adjust time to 30 minutes. When timer beeps, quick-release pressure until float valve drops and then unlock lid. Lift pan out of Instant Pot. Garnish immediately with chocolate chips and chopped peanuts. Let cool at room temperature for 10 minutes.
6. The cheesecake will be a little jiggly in the center. Refrigerate for a minimum of 2 hours to allow it to set. Release side pan and serve with drizzled chocolate syrup and whipped cream.

Orange New York Cheesecake

Servings: 6

Cooking Time: 1 Hour + Freezing Time

Ingredients:

- For the crust
- 1 cup graham crackers crumbs
- 2 tbsp butter, melted
- 1 tsp sugar
- For the filling
- 2 cups cream cheese
- ½ cup sugar
- 1 tsp vanilla extract
- Zest from 1 orange
- A pinch of salt
- 2 eggs

Directions:

1. Fold a 20-inch piece of aluminum foil in half lengthwise twice and set on the Instant Pot. Grease a parchment paper and line it to a cake pan. In a bowl, combine melted butter, sugar, and graham crackers. Press into the bottom and about ⅓ up the sides of the pan. Transfer the pan to the freezer as you prepare the filling.
2. In a separate bowl, beat sugar, cream cheese, salt, orange zest, and vanilla until smooth. Beat eggs into the filling, one at a time. Stir until combined. Add the filling over the chilled crust in the pan. Add 1 cup water and set a trivet into the pot. Put the pan on the trivet.
3. Seal the lid, press Cake, and cook for 40 minutes on High. Release the pressure quickly. Cool the cheesecake and then transfer it to the refrigerator for 3 hours. Use a paring knife to run along the edges between the pan and cheesecake to remove the cheesecake and set to the plate.

Spiced & Warming Mulled Wine

Servings: 6

Cooking Time: 20 Minutes

Ingredients:

- 3 cups red wine
- 2 tangerines, sliced
- ¼ cup honey
- 6 whole cloves
- 6 whole black peppercorns
- 2 cardamom pods
- 8 cinnamon sticks
- 1 tsp fresh ginger, grated
- 1 tsp ground cinnamon

Directions:

1. Add red wine, honey, cardamom, 2 cinnamon sticks, cloves, tangerine slices, ginger, and peppercorns. Seal the lid and cook for 5 minutes on High Pressure. Release pressure naturally for 10 minutes. Using a fine mesh strainer, strain the wine. Discard spices. Divide the warm wine into glasses. Garnish with cinnamon sticks to serve.

Chocolate Quinoa Bowl

Servings: 4

Cooking Time: 15 Minutes

Ingredients:

- 12 squares dark chocolate, shaved
- 2 tbsp cocoa powder
- 1 cup quinoa
- 2 tbsp maple syrup
- ½ tsp vanilla
- A pinch of salt
- 1 tbsp sliced almonds

Directions:

1. Put the quinoa, cocoa powder, maple syrup, vanilla, 2 ¼ cups water, and salt in your Instant Pot. Seal the lid, select Manual, and cook for a minute on High pressure. When ready, allow a natural release for 10 minutes and unlock the lid. Using a fork, fluff the quinoa. Top with almonds and dark chocolate and serve.

Butterscotch Crème Brûlée

Servings:4

Cooking Time: 20 Minutes

Ingredients:

- 4 large egg yolks
- 2 tablespoons sugar
- Pinch of salt
- ¼ teaspoon vanilla extract
- 1½ cups half-and-half
- ¾ cup butterscotch chips
- 2 cups water
- ½ cup superfine sugar

Directions:

1. In a small bowl, whisk together egg yolks, sugar, salt, and vanilla. Set aside.
2. In saucepan over medium-low heat, heat half-and-half until you reach a low simmer. Whisk a spoonful into the egg mixture to temper the eggs, then slowly add the egg mixture back into the saucepan with remaining half-and-half. Add butterscotch chips and continually stir on simmer until butterscotch is melted, about 10 minutes. Remove from heat and evenly distribute butterscotch mixture among four custard ramekins.
3. Pour water into Instant Pot. Insert trivet. Place silicone steamer basket onto trivet. Place ramekins onto steamer basket. Lock lid.
4. Press the Manual button and adjust time to 6 minutes. When the timer beeps, let pressure release naturally for 10 minutes. Quick-release any additional pressure until float valve drops and then unlock lid.
5. Transfer custards to a plate and refrigerate covered for 2 hours.
6. Right before serving, top custards with equal amounts superfine sugar. Blow-torch the tops to create a caramelized shell. Serve.

Measurement Conversions

BASIC KITCHEN CONVERSIONS & EQUIVALENT

DRY MEASUREMENTS CONVERSION CHART

3 TEASPOONS = 1 TABLESPOON = 1/16 CUP

6 TEASPOONS = 2 TABLESPOONS = 1/8 CUP

12 TEASPOONS = 4 TABLESPOONS = 1/4 CUP

24 TEASPOONS = 8 TABLESPOONS = 1/2 CUP

36 TEASPOONS = 12 TABLESPOONS = 3/4 CUP

48 TEASPOONS = 16 TABLESPOONS = 1 CUP

METRIC TO US COOKING CONVERSIONS

OVEN TEMPERATURE

120℃ = 250° F

160℃ = 320° F

180℃ = 350° F

205℃ = 400° F

220℃ = 425° F

OVEN TEMPERATURE

8 FLUID OUNCES = 1 CUP = 1/2 PINT = 1/4 QUART

16 FLUID OUNCES = 2 CUPS = 1 PINT = 1/2 QUART

32 FLUID OUNCES = 4 CUPS = 2 PINTS = 1 QUART = 1/4 GALLON

128 FLUID OUNCES = 16 CUPS = 8 PINTS = 4 QUARTS = 1 GALLON

BAKING IN GRAMS

1 CUP FLOUR = 140 GRAMS

1 CUP SUGAR = 150 GRAMS

1 CUP POWDERED SUGAR = 160 GRAMS

1 CUP HEAVY CREAM = 235 GRAMS

VOLUME

1 MILLILITER = 1/5 TEASPOON

5 ML = 1 TEASPOON

15 ML = 1 TABLESPOON

240 ML = 1 CUP OR 8 FLUID OUNCES

1 LITER = 34 FL. OUNCES

WEIGHT

1 GRAM = .035 OUNCES

100 GRAMS = 3.5 OUNCES

500 GRAMS = 1.1 POUNDS

1 KILOGRAM = 35 OUNCES

US TO METRIC COOKING CONVERSIONS

1/5 TSP = 1 ML

1 TSP = 5 ML

1 TBSP = 15 ML

1 FL OUNCE = 30 ML

1 CUP = 237 ML

1 PINT (2 CUPS) = 473 ML

1 QUART (4 CUPS) = .95 LITER

1 GALLON (16 CUPS) = 3.8 LITERS

1 OZ = 28 GRAMS

1 POUND = 454 GRAMS

BUTTER

1 CUP BUTTER = 2 STICKS = 8 OUNCES = 230 GRAMS = 8 TABLESPOONS

BUTTER

1 CUP = 8 FLUID OUNCES

1 CUP = 16 TABLESPOONS

1 CUP = 48 TEASPOONS

1 CUP = 1/2 PINT

1 CUP = 1/4 QUART

1 CUP = 1/16 GALLON

1 CUP = 240 ML

BAKING PAN CONVERSIONS

1 CUP ALL-PURPOSE FLOUR = 4.5 OZ

1 CUP ROLLED OATS = 3 OZ 1 LARGE EGG = 1.7 OZ

1 CUP BUTTER = 8 OZ

1 CUP MILK = 8 OZ

1 CUP HEAVY CREAM = 8.4 OZ

1 CUP GRANULATED SUGAR = 7.1 OZ

1 CUP PACKED BROWN SUGAR = 7.75 OZ

1 CUP VEGETABLE OIL = 7.7 OZ

1 CUP UNSIFTED POWDERED SUGAR = 4.4 OZ

BAKING PAN CONVERSIONS

9-INCH ROUND CAKE PAN = 12 CUPS

10-INCH TUBE PAN =16 CUPS

11-INCH BUNDT PAN = 12 CUPS

9-INCH SPRINGFORM PAN = 10 CUPS

9 X 5 INCH LOAF PAN = 8 CUPS

9-INCH SQUARE PAN = 8 CUPS

Recipe for:

Ingredients:

Equipment:

Description:

Instructions:

RECIPES

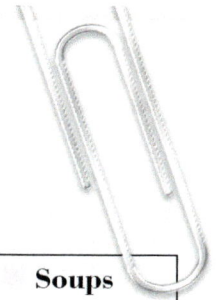

DATE

RECIPES	Salads	Meats	Soups
SERVES	Grains	Seafood	Snack
PREP TIME	Breads	Vegetables	Breakfast
COOK TIME	Appetizers	Desserts	Lunch
FROM THE KITCHEN OF	Main Dishes	Beverages	Dinners

INGREDIENTS

DIRECTIONS

NOTES

SERVING	☆☆☆☆☆
DIFFICULTY	☆☆☆☆☆
OVERALL	☆☆☆☆☆

Appendix : Recipes Index

Printed in Great Britain
by Amazon